Data Mapping for Data
Warehouse Design

Data Mapping for Data Warehouse Design

Qamar Shahbaz Ul Haq

ELSEVIER

AMSTERDAM • BOSTON • HEIDELBERG • LONDON
NEW YORK • OXFORD • PARIS • SAN DIEGO
SAN FRANCISCO • SINGAPORE • SYDNEY • TOKYO

Morgan Kaufmann is an imprint of Elsevier

Morgan Kaufmann is an imprint of Elsevier
225 Wyman Street, Waltham, MA 02451, USA

ISBN: 978-0-12-805185-6

British Library Cataloguing-in-Publication Data
A catalogue record for this book is available from the British Library

Library of Congress Cataloging-in-Publication Data
A catalog record for this book is available from the Library of Congress

For information on all Morgan Kaufmann publications
visit our website at www.mkp.com

Working together
to grow libraries in
developing countries

www.elsevier.com • www.bookaid.org

DEDICATION

To my parents,

    Ali Asghar and Inayat Begum,

who gave up everything in their lives for
my education and always believed in me.

CONTENTS

CHAPTER *1*

Introduction

Data mapping is the most important design step in the data warehouse lifecycle, and it impacts project success or failure. The process links the design and implementation phases of the project. The outcome of the process is the data mapping document, which is the main tool for communication between project designers and developers.

The data mapping document provides detailed steps in the data mapping process and provides a guide that a data mapper can use to successfully complete his or her task. The document also provides data mapping scenarios explaining different approaches to a problem and their pros and cons.

DEFINITION

Data mapping in a data warehouse is the process of creating a link between two distinct data models' (source and target) tables or attributes.

CHAPTER 2

Data Mapping Stages

Data mapping is required at many stages of the data warehouse life cycle; every stage has its own unique requirements and challenges. A data mapper's biggest challenge is to understand how data will flow from the source system to the final graphical user interface; this flow will determine how data should be transformed to achieve the end goal.

MAPPING FROM THE SOURCE TO THE DATA WAREHOUSE LANDING AREA

This kind of mapping is usually one to one, but may sometimes include transformations that can be done inside the source database engine. Such mapping helps by saving processing overhead toward the technology end of the architecture.

MAPPING FROM THE LANDING AREA TO THE STAGING DATABASE

Mapping from the landing area to the staging area is done by:

1. Selecting a subset of columns from the complete source file
2. Splitting a single column into multiple columns
3. Using information coming from the header or trailer for different purposes to cast the timestamp or date values to match the Target Database formats and so on.

MAPPING FROM THE STAGING DATABASE TO THE LOAD READY OR TARGET DATABASE

In this stage of the data warehouse lifecycle, source data is transformed into data warehouse data; data from here onward will be treated as information. This is why maximum importance, resources, and time should be given to this stage of data mapping. This book highlights various data mapping techniques for this stage.

The rules at this point can be complex and may involve multiple tables or sources. The rules here are governed by the vision that the data modeler has in mind about the data in a logical data model (LDM). All kinds of data integrations, history handling, data joining, lookups, reference data population, data-type conversion, and so on should be documented here. Usually this kind of data mapping is referred to as source matrix (SMX) or detail transformation design (DTD).

MAPPING FROM LOGICAL DATA MODEL TO THE SEMANTIC OR ACCESS LAYER

Data mapping LDM to the semantic, access, or PL layer involves data transformation to bring data into a state where business users can run reports and use the data as information. We will discuss this kind of data mapping in this chapter; however, Chapter 12 maps data for a scenario involving PL attributes in LDM.

CHAPTER *3*

Data Mapping Types

There are two types of data mapping done in any data warehouse project. High-level logical data mapping is part of the data modeling process, and implementation-oriented physical data mapping is used to document the transformation rule in detail.

LOGICAL DATA MAPPING

After the logical data model (LDM) is complete, the data mapper will start mapping source elements to LDM. This is high-level mapping and provides a baseline for more detailed physical mappings; the rules written are related more to logical concepts than to implementation.

PHYSICAL DATA MAPPING

When the physical data model is complete, the data mapper will write physical mappings or would physicalize the logical mappings written earlier. Here more detailed rules are needed that convey the mapper's vision of the data to the ETL (extract, transform, load) developer.

In this book, we will only discuss physical data mapping.

CHAPTER 4

Data Models

Before we go into a detailed discussion about data mapping, we need to understand the work that has been done before data mapping starts. The sequence in which a project usually flows is described in Figure 4.1.

A data mapper needs to understand the data model of the project to be able to make correct data mappings. The model might contain different forms of modeling techniques and require special considerations for certain entities or tables.

The data modeler starts by modeling the client's real-life objects into high-level concepts. This will result in a conceptual model; it can be high level or a relatively detailed one. Here the data modeler will not add any columns and might club many tables into a single concept. For example, the data modeler can group an employee, personal details, history, and so on into one concept employee (Figure 4.2).

The next step in the modeling process is to identify logical entities in the client's business, add attributes for each entity, and create relationships among entities. This generates a logical data model of the business that represents all entities of the business. This model will have complete information from a logical representation perspective, and it will provide the primary keys of every table, domain for each attribute, and so on.

After the logical model is complete, the modeler creates a physical data model using the client's actual source data and looking at the client's business requirements. The physical data model can roll up or roll down entities based on real requirements; similarly, not-required entities or columns can be deleted.

The physical data model will also define performance-related aspects such as indexes, partitioning, compression, and so on.

DEFINITION

The logical data model (LDM)/entity-relationship (ER) model is a data model for reporting and explaining the statistics and database elements

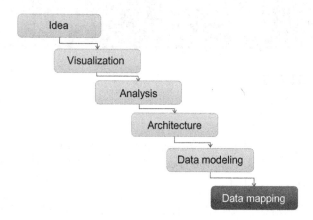

Figure 4.1 Data warehouse design steps.

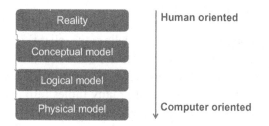

Figure 4.2 Data model types for data warehouse.

of a business sector or the demands for its procedures and techniques in an intellectual and theoretical manner that eventually leads to application in a database (e.g., a correlation database). The central elements of ER models are the entities and the relationships shared by them.

The ER model uses a methodical and well-ordered procedure to illustrate and outline a particular area of the business data. The data is expressed as features and characteristics that are connected to each other by associations that portray the necessities among them.

Entity-relationship models are illustrated using an ER diagram, which makes use of three elementary visual graphic symbols to exemplify and symbolize the data: entity, relationship, and attribute (Figure 4.3).

Entity

An entity is primarily interpreted as a place, an item, or a person of attention to a business or an establishment. An entity demonstrates a

Two-related entities

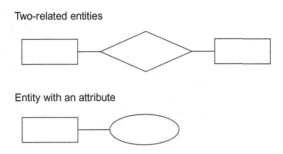

Entity with an attribute

Figure 4.3 Relationship of data model graphical illustration.

category of items, which in the actual world are objects that can be noticed and organized according to their features and qualities. Entities might consist of numerous different characteristics that categorize them.

In ER modeling, it is necessary to name and outline the entities to enable an uncomplicated and comprehensible interpretation and correspondence. Generally, the name of the entity is represented morphologically as a noun instead of a verb. The name of the entity is chosen based on how much it represents the attributes and elements of the entity. The most crucial job in ER modeling while designing an entity is to identify a candidate key. Such keys identify the data of entities uniquely and give them identification. The primary key is one of the candidate keys that is used often. For example, a person's candidate keys might include social security number, passport number, mobile number, or any other unique identification. When choosing a primary key, we might use social security number as primary key, because it is used most frequently.

An entity is classified as an item that has the ability to have an individualistic actuality that is distinctively recognizable. When we talk about an entity, we generally mean a feature of the actual world that can be differentiated from the other features of the world.

Relationship

A relationship is demonstrated by using lines drawn in between the entities. It portrays the structural communication and relationship between the entities in a model. A link is appointed morphologically using a verb. Figure 4.4 shows an ER diagram.

Apart from connecting line and name, we also need to include cardinality of a relationship. This gives a binding number that is shared between

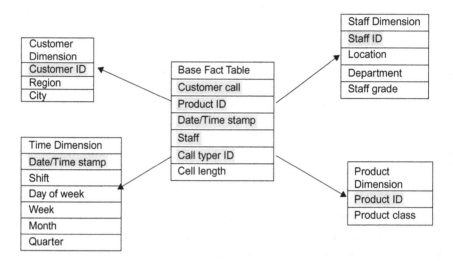

Figure 4.4 Relationships between fact and dimensions.

both entities. The options include one-to-one (both entities will have only one row for a Primary Key Foreign Key link), one-to-many (parent table will contain one row for the primary key, but the child table may contain multiple rows for relating foreign key column(s)), and many-to-many (both tables may contain multiple rows for shared key column(s)).

A top-level and influential ER diagram has names for the relationships; however, in a circumstantial and comprehensive ER diagram, generally connecting objects interpret the name of the relationship. The relationship is demonstrated by a line drawn in between the "component" and "product components." The annotations highlight the cardinality.

Whenever an entity's relationship is associated to itself, the relationship is said to be recurrent. Such relationships can be established using an associative entity or by keeping the foreign key from the same table's primary key. An example could be an employee table, where we need to keep the manager id. Since the manager is also an employee, we can either create a new associative table 'Employee Manager' having two foreign keys from employee or we can create a foreign key 'Manager id' linked with the primary key of the same table (employee id).

If the relationship has dependency between two entities, we need to load the primary key of the parent table as part of the composite primary key of the child table. For example, the Employee Address table will contain Employee Id (primary key of Employee table) as part of its own Primary key.

Attributes

Attributes demonstrates the features of the characteristics of the entities. In the example used, the description, product ID, and picture are attributes of the product entity. The attribute-naming customs are crucial. The name of an attribute must be distinctive in the entity and should be unambiguous and self-evident. For example, just mentioning date 1 and date 2 is not acceptable; rather, a clear and understandable definition is required, such as order and delivery date.

NORMALIZED DATA MODEL

For enterprise data warehouse, a normalized model in third normal form is the best option for the data model. Although relational integrities are not forced in the model, they are maintained using ETL (extract, transform, load) processes, keeping data connected within the model.

Third normal form data models are normally used for companies with large amounts of data and multiple source systems requiring data consolidation and complex business queries. There are performance-related constraints with 3NF models, but the benefits of having data stored in this form are far greater than the performance impact. Second, performance can be optimized using well-defined techniques from industry.

Below is a basic definition of the first three normal forms with examples.

First Normal Form

A table is in the first normal form (1NF) if

- The table has a primary key.
- No single column has multiple values.
- The nonprimary key columns depend on the primary key.

Second Normal Form

The second normal form applies to a table if

- The table satisfies 1NF (first normal form).
- Non-primary key attributes depend on all attributes of a composite key.

Third Normal Form

The third normal form applies to a table if

- The table meets the criteria for 2NF.

- Each nonprimary key attribute in a row does not depend on the entry in another key column.

DIMENSIONAL DATA MODEL

Dimensional modeling (DM) includes the procedures and conceptions used in data warehousing. It is believed to be disparate from ER modeling. DM does not consist of a correlated database. At an analytical level, the DM technique can be used for any substantial form, such as a multidimensional database or even unproductive files.

Dimensional modeling invariably uses the conceptions of dimensions and facts. Usually the facts are numerical values that can be summarized, and dimensions are divisions of rankings and illustrators that outline the facts.

In certain aspects, DM is uncomplicated, more costly, and simpler to interpret than ER modeling. However, dimension modeling is a comparatively up-to-date idea that is not vigorously defined in details, when compared with ER modeling.

Dimensional modeling has numerous fundamental concepts:

- Facts
- Dimensions
- Measures

Fact

A fact is made up of associated data items, including estimates and context data. Each aspect and feature demonstrate a business object, a business negotiation, or an occasion that can be used in interpreting the business or business procedures and techniques. In a data warehouse, facts are administered in the tables that consist of all the numerical data and information.

Dimension

Dimension is an integration of the representatives or components of the same sorts of perspectives. A dimension is generally expressed as an axis in a diagram. In DM, each data point in the fact table is related to one and only one associate from each of the multifarious dimensions. That is, dimensions regulate the contextual framework for the facts. Numerous analytic techniques are used to quantify the influence of the dimensions on the facts and features.

Dimensions are the boundaries over which we want to perform the OLAP (Online Analytic Processing). For example, to interpret the product sales in a database, the common dimensions could include:

- Employees
- Customers
- Time
- Location
- Budget

Measure
A measure is the mathematical aspect of a fact, illustrating the presentation or performance of the business in contrast to the dimensions. The real numbers are referred to as *variables*. For example, measures are the transactions in money, the measure of transactions, expenses of the supply, and quantities of the sales. A measure is classified by the integration of the associates of the dimensions and is placed on the facts.

Drill-Down and Roll-Up
Drill-down and roll-up are procedures for moving perspective up and down following the dimensional ranking levels. With the drill-down potential and ability, users move on to the higher levels of details. With the roll-up technique, users can zoom out to visualize a condensed measure of data. The route of navigation is regulated by the rankings within the dimensions. A roll-up performance is illustrated by Figure 4.5.

Roll-up is accomplished through ascending a conceptual ranking for the dimension position. Primarily, the conceptual ranking or hierarchy was "street < city < province < country." When we roll up a dimension, data is summarized to a higher level. In this case we are summarizing data (from a city to country) to get a high-level picture. In roll-up, one or multiple dimensions are removed from the report.

A roll-down is performed when we want to see more details of a summary report. (Figure 4.6 shows a roll-down.) In other words, we are moving down the hierarchy (in this example, for time hierarchy). The concept of time has two levels: Year (higher level) and Quarter (lower level). When we drill down, we are adding dimensions to

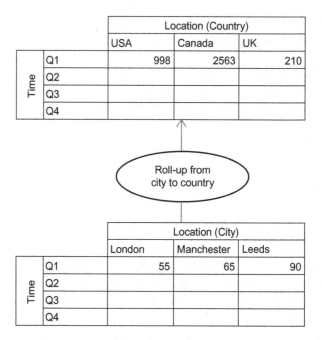

Figure 4.5 Roll-up from city to country.

summary data, making it relatively more detailed. This steers the data from not very detailed data to extremely elaborative data.

STAR SCHEMA

Numerous business administration data warehouses use the dimensional model in which a primary fact table holding the data (e.g., sales or support calls) is encompassed and associated with other fact tables including the dimensions of the fact table.

The star schema framework is the most straightforward form of the data mart schema. It consists of one or more fact tables with reference to dimension tables. The star schema is considered a special case of the snowflake and is more functional and constructive for tackling easy and simple inquiries.

The star schema framework is the most manageable and uncomplicated data warehouse schema. It is referred to as *star schema* because its diagram is similar to a star, with several different marks and spots diverging from the origin. The fact table is located in the middle of the star, and the different branches of the star are known as

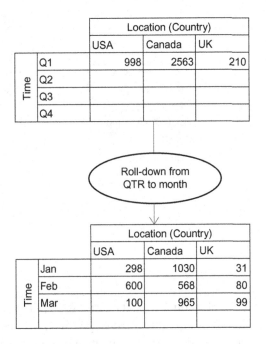

Figure 4.6 Roll-down from quarter (QTR) to month.

dimension tables. Normally, the fact tables of the star schema are present in the 3NF, and the dimensional tables are denormalized. Even though the star schema is the easiest approach, it is not much used these days.

The star schema distinguishes the data into facts, which include all the numerical data; the dimensions are the illustrative and graphical aspects of the facts.

Fact Tables

A fact table may consist of data of the facts in detail and totality. A fact table stores quantitative information for analysis and may consist of data of the facts in detail/totality. Generally there are two separate columns in a fact table: foreign key to dimension tables and measures.

Dimension Tables

A dimension is a constitution and a framework that is normally comprised of one or more than one ranking or scale used for grouping and designating the data. A dimension that lacks any hierarchy or ranking is known as a *flat dimension*. Each dimension table has its own primary keys, which are a constituent of the composite primary key of

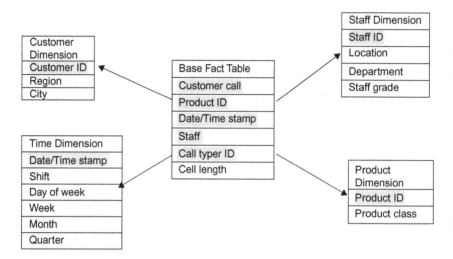

Figure 4.7 Relationships between fact and dimensions.

the fact table. The dimensional aspects assist in explaining the value of dimension. Usually, they are illustrative, pictorial values. In size, the dimension tables are usually more compact than fact tables.

Whereas a normal fact table holds the data and information on sales, a dimension table stores the data relevant to the geographical location, consumers, timings, and products.

A star schema has the following features:

- It is uncomplicated and easily understandable.
- It has substantial inquiry effectiveness and a small number of tables to join.
- It is most frequently used up in data warehouse administration and is assisted by numerous business comprehension devices.

In Figure 4.7, the fact table consists of four fundamental dimensions: customer, product, time, and staff. All of these dimensions are associated with the fact table by indexes (the highlighted parts) to allow the tables to be linked and to permit fast queries and data interpretations.

This data model is uncomplicated, enables rapid recovery, and can be easily understood without alternating all the current regular reports and inquiries. A disadvantage to this model is that there is some data dismissal, which can potentially result in irregularity if all of the redundant data is kept up-to-date.

CHAPTER 5

Data Mapper's Strategy and Focus

A data mapper is the person responsible for mapping source data on target data.

MAPPER WHO? HOW DOES HE OR SHE DO IT?

Let's take an example. Consider a paper game that we used to enjoy playing in childhood, connect the dots. In Figure 5.1, it is very clear and easy to connect one dot to the other because every dot is numbered.

But what if the numbering is missing against the dots (Figure 5.2)? We may still be able to complete the picture and prove that this is a picture of a flower. There is a chance of making mistakes, but eventually we may be able to conclude that this is what we think of as a flower.

Now let us consider Figure 5.3. In a real-life situation, this is the starting point for a data mapper. A data mapper identifies actual dots to be connected by getting guidance from logical data model (LDM)/ physical data model (PDM), meeting subject matter experts (SMEs), profiling data, and other means.

Let's assume that with guidance and support, the mapper identifies the connection between the dots and finally comes up with something that looks like Figure 5.4.

If the data mapper is asked to present his or her opinion based on the above picture, he or she might assume that it's an elephant. The word "assume" is very dangerous in data mapping; assumptions can cause errors that might be identified at a much later stage that may result in a lot of rework.

With a few more discussions with SME, more dots are identified and connected (Figure 5.5).

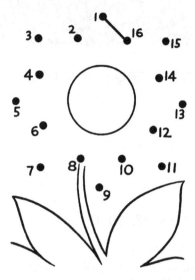

Figure 5.1 Connect the dots example with labels.

Figure 5.2 Connect the dots example without labels.

The dots may look like a giraffe now; again, it is just an assumption.

Assumptions should be avoided. Every time we make an assumption, it will come back as rework.

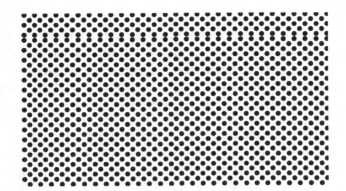

Figure 5.3 Connect the dots example with no clues.

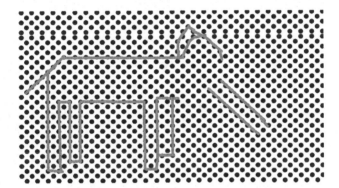

Figure 5.4 Results of the data mapper's analysis.

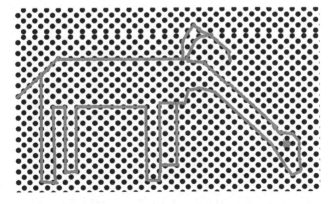

Figure 5.5 The data mapper identifies the correct concept with further analysis.

A data mapper must perform detailed analysis and data profiling to avoid assumptions. Usually we have to rely on assumptions when the client SME or source data model is missing. In such cases, data mappers should use other methods for an accurate decision-making capability. Assumptions might make us feel comfortable for a while, but they may be hazardous in the longer run.

The SME is the best source of information for data mappers because it helps to provide source documentation and explanations. The SME should be available to data mappers until the design of the project is complete. To fabricate an optimum and reliable data mapping document, the data mapper and data modeler should sit with the SME at same location to hold effective communication.

CHAPTER *6*

Uniqueness of Attributes and its Importance

The uniqueness of an item gives it identity in its environment. A person living in a country is identified by his or her unique social security number; this identity differentiates him or her from the rest of the people living in the same country. It enables the person to get a bank account, home and car registration, job, and so on.

Uniqueness is mandatory in the real world and may be defined by the level of uniqueness depending on its environment, organization, locale, and so on. For example, in an office, every employee is uniquely identified; however, glasses are not uniquely identified. The reason is that the company does not need to track the activities of the glasses or cups. They do not hold a high value to the company, and a breakage is insignificant in terms of cost to the company.

Can we say the same about laptops? Every company keeps track of laptops given to its employees and uses a service tag to identify them uniquely. The reason for identifying a laptop uniquely is to ensure that it can be tracked for administrative purposes and claiming a warranty from the supplier in case of a breakdown.

Similarly, in data warehousing, we must understand the level of uniqueness that a company maintains.

The uniqueness of three industries is highlighted in this chapter.

TELECOM

In the telecom industry, a connection is identified by a mobile number; however, the hierarchy is of multiple levels.

Level 1 = Customer:
Uniquely identified by customer ID. XYZ company is customer of Orange UK and is uniquely identified by customer number = TD123

Level 2 = Subscriber:
Uniquely identified by account number (not by mobile number because it can change on request) account number = 2389749
Level 3 = Subscription:
A subscription is a product subscriber by a user (account holder) and is uniquely identified by product ID

At each level, uniqueness is mandatory because it is required for billing and other purposes. One can assume that a connection is uniquely identified by a mobile number, however same mobile number can be given to a new customer once old customer's connection is closed. Both mobile number and SIM number (IMSI) for a connection can change; hence, they do not provide the necessary uniqueness required to run the business.

MANUFACTURING

Let's take an example of a car manufacturer. Let's assume that CAR_MAKER uniquely identifies a car by giving it a companywide unique ID.

Level 1 = Batch:
All cars of type Civic come in one match, so a batch is identified uniquely. Batch number = 2013_CIVI_HYBRID_EUII
Level 2 = Car:
All cars within a batch are given a unique chassis number. Chassis = HSU_HJKSJK_72373
Level 3 = Engine:
Because an engine can be replaced during the lifecycle of a car, it is necessary to give it a unique ID. Engine number = 8978977

Note here that CAR_MAKER's internal car ID is useful to CAR_MAKER, but when it comes to global operations and car usage, the chassis number identifies each car uniquely. When a car is registered in any country, the chassis number will be used rather than CAR_MAKER's own identification. Also, an engine has unique identification because it requires repairing or replacing.

There could be more examples of manufacturers that want identification of other car parts as well. For example, CAR_MAKER_2 might give unique identifications to doors, suspension, seats, and so on. CAR_MAKER_2 might be looking to give better "after-sale services" to its users by knowing which supplier provided a faulty component, which factory worker installed the component, at what time the component was installed, which production line assembled the car, and so on.

FINANCE

In the financial sector, let's take example of a bank FI_BANK. A bank identifies an account by an account number.

Level 1 = Customer
Uniquely identified by a SSN number = SD12383-1980
Level 2 = Account
Uniquely identified by an account number = 323-2323321-98
Level 2 = Credit card
Uniquely identified by a credit card number = 8977645282726

UNIQUENESS IN DATA WAREHOUSE

More unique identification means more control over business; however, uniqueness has costs associated with it such as IT servers, software licenses, and data entry at every point the item is used (supplier, testing, assembly, quality check). Each company must make its own decision about level of uniqueness based on its business model and the costs associated with uniqueness.

If we talk about data warehouse, the more unique the level of data, the better the reporting capability for business users. At the same time, it requires more work in design and implementation.

The data mapper must identify every table in source by its unique primary key; similarly, every table in the logical data model should have a unique primary key.

The data mapper should also know which columns he or she needs to use to get unique data when there are multiple rows for the same primary key. This is one of the biggest challenges in data mapping and requires the subject matter expert's input along with data profiling to identify the correct column to get the correct data from staging to the target area.

For history handling, there are two levels of uniqueness to understand. Number one is the primary key of the overall table, which is a list of columns that make a row unique. Number two is the list of columns that requires history handling if they change. For example, Employee Address might have a unique primary key made up of Employee ID and Address_Start_date; however, change of address will be checked for Employee ID only.

CHAPTER 7

Prerequisites of Data Mapping

Before someone starts data mapping, he or she must have access to the following.

LOGICAL DATA MODEL

The first thing a data mapper needs to refer to is the logical data model (LDM) of the project. This is the target he or she will be mapping the data on. To accomplish this task, the data mapper needs to analyze the following items within LDM.

ENTITIES AND THEIR DESCRIPTION

The data mapper must understand every entity and its intended purpose in LDM. He or she should also classify entities into history, master, transaction, reference, data warehouse maintained, and associative entities.

ATTRIBUTES AND THEIR DESCRIPTION

In a data warehouse, most entities and attributes' names are kept generic so they can be used for multiple types of data and to maintain business concepts of the organization rather than source-specific names. This means that the data mapper should understand an attribute's purpose in the entity. The description of the column provides necessary information about the attribute. For example, Party_Id is a unique ID that will identify a party. A party can be an employee, customer, supplier, shop, and so on.

Primary Key of Entities

As discussed in Chapter 6, the primary key must be defined for every entity in the data warehouse LDM. Primary keys are usually well defined in all logical data models; however, data mappers must understand why certain columns become part of a primary key (e.g., entities that have multiple columns in the primary key, especially history and associative entities).

Another usage of primary key is in natural keys and surrogate keys. If the solution architect of the project has decided to use surrogate keys, then you will find a single column in most master entities such as party (Party_Id) and address (Address_Id). However, if natural keys have been used for the primary key of the table, then you will find multiple attributes in the primary key of the table. For example, in the party table, there could be two attributes of the primary key, that is, Party_Id mapped from the source and Party_Type_Cd to uniquely identify the parties if different sources for this table are using the same type of party ID. For example, the supplier management department and finance department both could be using numeric IDs: 751 can be the ID for the supplier as well as for an employee. Within the sources, they are unique, but when we bring both types of data into the party table of the data warehouse, there will a problem with uniqueness.

Relationship Between Entities

Relationships within two entities are well defined and are usually named. Understanding relationships is important because sometimes the data mapper is not familiar with the industry for which the project is being implemented. Analyzing relationships will give thorough business understanding of the organization. For example, consider Figure 7.1. The sales order will have information about the order given to the organization by a customer, and an invoice is generated when a product is delivered. The relationship here says that a sales order has

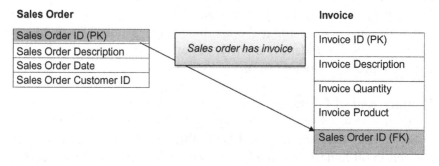

Figure 7.1 Relationship name between two tables.

an invoice. In other words, an invoice will be generated against the sales order.

Cardinality of the Relationship

In Chapter 6, we discussed the example of the telecom sector. We saw that a customer can have more than one connection to the telecom company. For example, a company might provide an official connection to all its employees. Therefore, cardinality between the customer and employee is one to many.

Similarly, every employee can get multiple subscriptions from the telecom operator. Therefore, cardinality between the subscriber and subscription is one to many. However, if a subscription is identified by a unique ID only, and its instance is not assigned a unique ID, then the cardinality between the two will be many to many.

Change Capture Column of History-Handled Entities

In history-handled entities, the data mapper should identify the entity for which change will be tracked. Usually history-handled entities have multiple columns depending on logic.

In such cases, it is ideal to identify the list of columns for which change in other columns will occur as a result of closing an older row and opening a new record.

PHYSICAL DATA MODEL

A physical data model (PDM) study is equally important during the data mapping process. PDM gives information about entities that have rolled up from the LDM, primary indexes, data types of attributes, secondary indexes, partitioning, compressing, journaling, fallback, character set, and so on.

All mappings from the source will be made to the PDM target tables. The transformation rules are also based on PDM data types and so on.

The PDM is also important because in certain mappings, we will have to join the source table with target tables; in such cases, the primary index (PI) of the source and target table should be known to have some idea of performance of queries.

SOURCE SYSTEM DATA MODEL

In most projects, the source entity or attribute list is considered enough for data mapping. However, the source data model is necessary for understanding the source data. Just like data warehouse LDM, source LDM provides information about relationships, primary keys, cardinality, and so on.

It is absolutely mandatory to identify the primary key of all source tables. Without this information, there can be duplicates in data, and the data mapper will not be able to write correct rules. Having the exact primary key of the source entity will help the data mapper create a rule (rank, qualify, group by) to select distinct data out of duplicates (which can happen because of multiple day extracts or any other reason).

SOURCE SYSTEM TABLE AND ATTRIBUTE DETAILS

Usually during data modeling, stage source system tables and their attributes are listed down, and high-level mapping is also done giving the target table where the attribute will be mapped.

The exact data type, character set, compression, indexes, and so on are necessary to create the data mapping document.

SUBJECT MATTER EXPERT

The subject matter expert (SME) provides detailed information about the source and answers all questions from the data warehouse team. The SME will also provide required documentation about the source and can give information about issues that are not documented or may need special treatment. Good SME availability can result in a high-quality data mapping document.

PRODUCTION QUALITY DATA

Last, production quality data should be available to the data mapper for profiling and analysis. The data mapper will run queries against the data for making rules. If the data sample does not represent real data, then transformation rules will be wrong, and the project will be affected.

CHAPTER 8

Surrogate Keys versus Natural Keys

One of the key decisions in data warehouse architecture is about selecting primary keys for the tables. The decision is made based on multiple factors, such as:

- Performance
- Data quality
- Extract, transform, load (ETL) architecture
- Metadata management
- Space
- New system integration

We will not discuss this here because the decision is made by the solution architect, and the data mapper has to follow the guidelines irrespective of the decision made. In this chapter, we discuss the impact of data mapping on both types of keys, natural and surrogate.

NATURAL KEYS

Natural keys make data mapping very easy and controllable. The mapping is done one to one from the source to the target.

However, missing information means that the data mapper will have to make special rules to allow such data into the logical data model (LDM). For example, consider that sales data is loaded into the LDM SALES table (PK/PI = sale_id), and sale_id is missing for 2000 of 10,000 rows. In this case, the data mapper will have to make a dummy sale_id so that data can be populated into the LDM SALES table.

SURROGATE KEYS

Surrogate keys require one additional step in the ETL process and similarly, one additional mapping from the source for every key. There is also dependency in the ETL process during execution; the surrogate key should be generated before it is used in subsequent mappings.

Special rules are required to handle missing data if other sources are providing the data. Surrogate keys can help significantly if multiple identifications are available for the same concept.

CHAPTER 9

Data Mapping Document Format

After the data mapper has analyzed everything and has made a decision about the mapping, he or she needs to document the mapping. Word and Excel documents are used mostly depending on the need of the project.

We will use an Excel file for documenting all the rules. Let's divide every mapping into two sections.

HEADER-LEVEL RULES

For better documentation and communication to the ETL team, all rules related to table joining, filtering, and qualifying should be documented in the header. In other words, anything that will come after the "FROM" part of SQL should be documented here.

COLUMN-LEVEL RULES

All column-level rules are documented in front of every attribute. These rules may include data type casting, ranking, case statements, NULL value handling, timestamp manipulation, data split, and so on.

MAJOR PARTS OF THE DATA MAPPING DOCUMENT

Following are the major parts of the data mapping document.

1. Change log: Gives details of the changes done in the current release
2. Mapping tracker: Gives a list of mappings and a small description
3. Legend: Gives details of the color scheme or any other method used
4. Data mappings: Actual mappings
5. Reference data: Constant values defined by data warehouse for types, roles, reasons, and other reference codes (separate document)
6. Loading dependency: Defines the source system level loading dependency

DATA MAPPING COLUMNS EXPLAINED

See Figure 9.1.

Change Date

This column contains the date when the rule is changed and a row marker (N, U, or D). N stands for new, U for update, and D for deleted mapping or row.

Subject Area

Subject area from the logical data model (LDM): If the target table shares multiple subject areas, then ask the data modeler to identify the most relevant areas.

Target Table Name

Target table name from physical data model (PDM)

Target Column Name

Target column name from PDM

Data Type

Data type of target column from PDM

PK

Is this column the primary key in logical data model (LDM)? Use Y for yes and N for no.

Nullable

Is this column nullable? Use Y for yes and N for no.

Source System

This is the source system from which this mapping is sourced. There can be two sources in certain cases. Use the source system that is providing data for the primary key of the target table.

Record ID

The record ID uniquely identifies the mapping for a target table. For example, the PARTY target table can have three mappings from the same source; the record ID will be EMS001, EMS002, and EMS003.

Change Date	Target Table Name	Target column Name	Date Type	PK	Null/Able	Source System	Record Id	Source Table Name	Source column Name	Transformatio n Category	Transformation Role	Updated By
N.2013-05-01	Party					EMS	EMS001	Employee Employee_Status			+ Joing Employee with Employee_Status on Employee_Id	
N.2013-05-01	Party	Party_Id	Integer	Y	N	EMS	EMS001	Employee	Employee_Id	Direct		John
N.2013-05-01	Party	Party_Name	VARCHAR(50)	N	Y	EMS	EMS001	Employee	Employee_Name	Direct		John
N.2013-05-01	Party	Party_Desc	VARCHAR(50)	N	Y	EMS	EMS001	Constant	NULL	Hardcode		John
N.2013-05-01	Party	Party_Status	Integer	N	Y	EMS	EMS001	Employee_Status	Status_Cd	Transformation		John
N.2013-05-01	Party	Party_Type_Cd	Integer	N	Y	EMS	EMS001	Constant	'Internal Employee'	Lookup		John
N.2013-05-01	Party	Party_Active_Ind	Smallint	N	Y	EMS	EMS001	Employee	Active_Date	Transformation	Case When Expiry_Date > Current_Date than 1 else 0	John
N.2013-05-01	Party	Source	VARCHAR(50)	N	Y	EMS	EMS001	Constant	'EMS'	Hardcode		John
N.2013-05-01	Party	Load_Time	Timestamps(0)	N	Y	EMS	EMS001	ETL	Current_Time	Hardcode		John

Figure 9.1 Data mapping example.

Source Table Name

This is the name of the source table from which the data will be loaded into this target table. If no column from the source is used, then write

ETL: for all values that are populated during the loading process such as Current_Timestamp

CONTANT: if a hardcoded value is used or a lookup is made from another table based on a constant

If two tables' columns are used from the source, then write both tables' names.

Source Column Name

This is the column names whose value will be loaded into the target column. If two columns are used, then write both columns' name here. For constants (hardcoded and lookups), enclose them in quotes (e.g., "1").

Data Type of Source Column

Source database data type of the column.

Transformation Category

This column is very important for the ETL team that will develop the mappings. It categorizes every column based on its treatment in mapping. Possible values are:

- Direct: Direct mapping of course column; no transformation of any kind
- Transformation: There is some rule for this column; the actual rule is in the *Transformation Rule* column
- Hardcoded: Insert the hardcoded value in the *Source Column Name* column.
- Lookup: Use value in *Source Column Name* and look it up in table whose foreign key is in *Target Column Name*. The lookup will be on the description or name column, and the primary key column value will be used in mapping.

Transformation Rule

Here we document actual transformation rule for the column and provide all relevant details. It is good practice to write the rule in easy-to-understand words or in Pseudo SQL code. However when it is difficult to explain a rule in words, SQL code can be used.

Updated By

This column gives the data mapper's name that created or updated the mapping.

Mapping Priority or Sequence

This column gives the loading sequence of mappings (i.e., which mapping is loaded first and which afterward).

CHAPTER 10

Data Analysis Techniques

Earlier chapters have discussed the importance of getting maximum understanding of the data. After the data mapper knows the logical and physical details of the data, he or she can create good mapping.

Data can be understood using different techniques, starting from meetings with the subject matter expert (SME) to running SQL queries on the dataset. A data mapper is extremely lucky if he or she gets all the information from the client's SME, but this is not usually the case, and the data mapper must use different techniques for analyzing the data.

Analyzing source data requires a mind full of curiosity and the ability to dig deep. From standard approaches of data analysis to specialized case-based techniques, the data mapper spends most of his or her time analyzing data. The key rule here is to understand the data in totality and not leave anything on assumption.

This chapter discusses the tools, technologies, and techniques for data analysis.

SOURCE DATA SAMPLE

The first thing you need is access to the client's source data. A good amount of data sample will help you run different queries. A good data sample can be defined as the "amount of data that represents current and historic production data." *Representation* is vague term and should be defined after meeting with the client and getting an overview of the source.

For a transactional source system, a good data sample can be defined as X month's data for the past Y years. If the client migrated the source system in the past, then you need to have the same amount of data from the old source. X and Y can be mutually agreed on with the client. Normally, if you are taking data from all previous years, then 1 month per year is sufficient, but there can be cases in which 1 month might not be enough. For example, a retailer would have a large number of transactions around Christmas and the summer sales time.

Organizations with large amounts of data change their operational (OLTP) systems often for many reasons. When analyzing data, you should have access to all previous systems if history data is required to meet business requirements.

For the master data of the client, it is good practice to get the complete dataset. This data will be joined many times, and missing data might result in wrong results.

Direct Access

The best scenario is when the client gives direct access to the source system. For example, if the client is using MSSQL (Microsoft SQL Database Engine) for its source, they can provide a user and a work database in which the analyst can create temporary tables for analysis.

Sometimes getting this kind of access is not possible because of security or other reasons. Another reason could be avoiding heavy queries on the operational system; service providers usually have SLA agreements and do not allow such analysis queries to be executed on a source.

Getting access to the source system can have a big impact on the success of the project.

Extraction from a Source

Most of the time, the client will provide read-only access to its source system, and you are allowed to load data in a given time window.

The data warehouse team can create a connection with the source and bring data to their own database. Further analysis can be done on the data warehouse database.

Data Files

The last option for receiving a data sample is in files provided by the client. These files may have a limited amount of data that does not fulfill analysis requirements; nevertheless, these files provide the best possible situation.

In this kind of situation, it is good practice to first analyze the available source data and then request specific data from the client based on results. After confidence is built, more data can be requested from the client.

WHAT TO LOOK FOR

The data mapping process starts with understanding of all source systems and how they connect with each other. An enterprise data warehouse is only beneficial if information from different sources is combined to give a single picture of the organization. Hence, it is very important to verify the connection using actual data.

High-Level Inter-Source System Relationship

The client provides documentation that describes the source system, and a fruitful meeting can help the data mapper understand the connection between different sources. Because you have sample data available, start running SQL queries.

Consider that we are making a data warehouse for a bank, and it has two sources. The first source, ACC (Accounts), gives the master data for an account holder and the second source, TRN (transactions), provides details of daily transactions.

From an analysis point of view, both sources should connect based on account number; that is, a transaction can only be done if the customer already has a bank account, and an account must have at least one transaction because the customer opened an account.

Start by joining both tables.

```
Select
  SUM (CASE WHEN DISTINCT(A.account_no) IS NOT NULL AND
DISTINCT(B.account_no) IS NOT NULL THEN 1 ELSE 0) AS FOUND_IN_BOTH,
  SUM (CASE WHEN DISTINCT(B.account_no) is NULL THEN 1 ELSE 0) AS
FOUND_ONLY_IN_ACC,
  SUM (CASE WHEN DISTINCT(A.account_no) is NULL THEN 1 ELSE 0) AS
FOUND_ONLY_IN_TRN,
FROM
  ACC A
FULL OUTER JOIN
  TRN B
ON A.account_no = B.account_no;
```

Table 10.1 Result of the Query		
FOUND_IN_BOTH	FOUND_ONLY_IN_ACC	FOUND_ONLY_IN_TRN
99000	100	50000

The above query should give you counts of data available in both systems; imagine the result looks like Table 10.1.

To further confirm the above stats, run the same query by trimming the account number.

```
 ON TRIM(A.account_no) = TRIM(B.account_no)
If stats stay same, remove trailing '0'
 ON TRIM(TRIM ( '0' from A.account_no)) = TRIM(TRIM ('0' from
B.account_no))
```

If the resultset is still the same, browse data from both sides and see if missing account_no values have something appended in the start. There is a possibility that the ACC system maintains numeric account numbers and the TRN system adds branch code in start. Even then the story doesn't end here; you keep on analyzing columns until you are 100% sure that something is missing.

After you have exhausted your options, your next approach should be to identify whether there is an issue of data sample completeness. As discussed earlier, the master data sample (account data in this case) should be the complete dataset from the source.

Run the below query to see if you received all historical account data.

```
SELECT account_opening_date, COUTN(*)
FROM ACC
GROUP BY 1
ORDER BY 1
```

The above query result should give you an idea how far back in history account data is available. If you see missing dates, then you can ask the client:

1. Is there a legacy system before the ACC source system? If yes, then provide the complete data sample.

2. Does the TRN source system maintain data for a nonaccounts source? For example, the TRN system might also maintain credit card transactions, which we won't find in ACC. If the answer is yes, then the client should provide other source systems data and a business rule to differentiate between two datasets.

Intra-Source System Table-Level Analysis

After a data mapper has established a high-level understanding of a source system, he or she should start looking into each table of the source system. The data mapper should look for:

1. **Table description:** Find out why this table exists in the source and what it logically means. What kind of data does it store? Is this table redundant for DWH, or will it serve some purpose in data mapping? Some tables in the source system can have a special purpose such as history handling; the data mapper needs to identify how source data will be transformed into information using data mapping.
2. **Table relationships:** Just like intersource relationship analysis, run SQL queries to identify or verify table relationships within a source. If a data mapper is lucky, the client will provide the logical data model (LDM) of the source, but if not, then the data mapper will run analysis queries to create a physical LDM or visualization. Without well-defined relationships, joins defined in data mapping can produce wrong results.
3. **Primary key:** Whether the client provided the primary key of the table or not, the data mapper should use SQL queries to identify or verify the primary key of the table.

```
SELECT C1, count (*)
FROM tbl
GROUP BY C1
HAVING COUNT (*) >1
```

If the above query returns a result, then it means that the C1 is not unique. Next you need to identify whether the table has a composite primary key or the data sample contains multiple extracts. We will discuss this in more detail in the uniqueness section of this chapter.

1. **Data generation scenarios:** Data in a source table comes from applications, and we need to understand why a new row is inserted

into the source table. In telecom organizations, a row is Call Detail Record (CDR) generated: A consumer makes a call, sends Short Message Service (SMS), uses the Internet, or performs other activities. There could be activities for which data is generated, but documentation is not available. For example, some telecom operators store missed calls, and some don't; some operators even track events such as registering of consumer connections with the network. Without getting a complete generation scenarios list, we cannot understand the source data properly.

2. **Data update and delete scenarios:** In most OLTP systems, data can be updated or even deleted (soft or hard). What are these scenarios? Does the source keep slowly changing dimension (SCD) logic for updates? Does the source physically delete rows or mark them as deleted?

Column-Level Analysis

Because columns are mapped from the source to the target, it is very important to analyze column values from both a logical and a physical perspective.

For logical understanding of the column values, SME can provide information that can be verified from the data. For the physical demographics of a column, we can write a generic query that will generate SQL queries for all columns of all tables of the source. This will result in a systematic approach toward data analysis and can provide an error-free resultset.

One example of such a query generator is given below, which gives the null count, distinct values, maximum length, and minimum length.

```
SELECT 'select '||''''''||trim(Column_Name)||' '||trim
(column_type)||' '||trim(length)||''''
    ||',sum(case when '||trim(Column_Name)||' is null then 1 else 0
end) as "Null Count" '
    ||',count(distinct '||trim(Column_Name)||') as "Distinct
Values" '
    ||',max(length('||trim(Column_Name)||')) as "Maximum Length" '
    ||',min(length('||trim(Column_Name)||')) as "Minimum Length" '
    ||'from dbo.Table_Name;' As "Profile Queries"
FROM information_Schema
WHERE database_name = 'Source_DB_Name';
```

Apart from this analysis, you can run other queries as well to better understand the column. Some time looking at the data helps identify strange and nondocumented values of the column. This can help in writing a better transformation rule that can handle all type of anomalies.

For all columns that have relationships with other tables' columns, you must join both tables and identify child data that is missing in the parent table. This missing data should be investigated further to understand why this data is present in the table.

UNIQUENESS

The most common problem in data mapping is incorrect primary key logic of source data. Sometimes we think that a certain column or columns define data uniquely, but they do not, resulting in logical and physical errors.

From a logical perspective, the wrong primary key results in missing or duplicated data in reports. This means that the main purpose of making a data warehouse is not fulfilled; wrong reports mean wrong decisions by management.

When doing table-level analysis, the first thing a data mapper should do is identify columns that uniquely define the table's data. Such columns (or a single column) are known as the primary key of the table. If the source primary key is correctly identified, then the resulting data mapping will serve the purpose.

Below are a few scenarios in which primary key duplication can occur and their solutions.

Full Row Duplicates

Full row duplicate data can be defined as a row or tuple that has the same value for every column. There are two possibilities of a full row duplicate occurrence:

1. **The source contains duplicates:** If the source is giving full row duplicates, then we need to identify the reason behind these duplicates. It could be an error in the source or there could be an explanation for this behavior of the data.

Table 10.2 Full Row Duplicate Example		
Item	Time	Cost
Eggs	10/10/2015 12:25	2.56
Eggs	10/10/2015 12:25	2.56

At first glance, of a full row duplicate from the source, we can classify it as an error in source, but there may be business logic behind such duplicates, and data mapping should handle such cases.

Let's create a hypothetical case; in real life you, will come across such issues. A grocery shop records all transactions when customers check out using old software that was meant for a single checkout counter. Over a period of time, the shop owner has had to add more counters as the customer number increases, but the store is using the same software.

Now if two customers buy the same item at exactly the same time, then we will get a full row duplicate (Table 10.2). If the LDM of the data warehouse doesn't allow these duplicates, then you need to request a modeler to change the primary key of the target table and add a surrogate counter.

This new counter can easily be generated using Rank/Row Number functions available in most DataBase Management Systems (DBMSs).

```
SELECT item, time, cost, RANK() OVER ( PARTITION BY item, time, cost
  ORDER BY time) as Transaction_Number
FROM tbl
```

On the other hand, the client can also confirm that these full row duplicates are actually an error in the source. In this case, either the client can take responsibility and clean the source or a rule can be added in the data mapping to clean the data.

For a full row duplicate, a simple DISTINCT can solve the problem:

```
SELECT DISTINCT item, time, cost
FROM tbl
```

Or a group by statement:

```
SELECT item, time, cost
FROM tbl
Group by item, time, cost
```

2. **Duplicates after table joins:** Sometimes in a mapping, we join multiple source tables to create a target dataset. If we identify such duplicates, then further analysis is needed to identify the correct primary key of the target table or to ignore duplicate rows.

Primary Key Duplicates

While doing data analysis of the table, we need to first identify the primary key of the table. If the client has already provided this information, then we need to confirm the primary key from the data.

Run the below query to see if the primary key is duplicated.

```
SELECT PK_columns, Count(*)
FROM tbl
GROUP BY PK_columns
HAVING count(*) > 1
```

The above query will group by all data for the same primary key columns and return a result if it finds more than one row for any primary key (PK) value. Getting a result for the above query means that either our PK is not correct or there is explanation for this duplication.

The first thing you need to do is to browse duplicated data and see if you can identify the root cause.

```
SELECT A.*
From tbl as A
INNER JOIN
(
  SELECT PK_Cols
  FROM
  (
    SELECT PK_Cols, Count(*) as C
    FROM tbl
```

```
    Group by PK_Cols
    HAVING C > 1
) ABC
) B
ON A.PK_Cols = B,PK_Cols
ORDER BY A.PK_Cols
```

Below are some reasons for PK duplicates and their solutions for data mapping.

Multiple Extracts

If the data sample contains multiple extracts of the same data, then qualify data based on the latest extract date or delete old extracts from the table for analysis. Deleting data is not a wise decision; this will be explained in the next scenario.

```
SELECT *
FROM tbl
QUALIFY ( RANK () OVER(PARTITION BY PK_Cols ORDER BY Extract_Ts)) = 1
```

Source System Updates

Sometimes the source updates data, and the results in two copies of the same row. The difference can be in any nonprimary key column. In such a case, the data mapper has to see how the data will be transformed in the target table. If the target table has the same primary key, then the data modeler needs to confirm that the latest row should be stored. If the target table has history maintenance columns, then these are not duplicates; in fact, they are useful for data warehousing because the history will be maintained. If the source provides a TimeStamp for the updated record, then it will be used for tracking history in DWH; if the source doesn't provide a time when change happened, then data warehouse extraction time will be used for maintaining history.

HISTORY PATTERN ANALYSIS

Source systems maintain history and might have implemented special logic different from conventional techniques. Understanding this data is very important to map data correctly; the data in the source might contain anomalies or might have some business reasoning.

Before we go into analysis details, let's first look at types of history handling techniques. These are usually referred to as SCD. Different types of techniques are explained in this section.

In a data warehouse, to report historical data, there is a requirement for pursuing modifications and following up changes in dimension attributes. This is where SCDs are used. These are dimensions that gradually change with time instead of changing systematically on a uniform program. Executing one of these SCD types allows the users to allocate the appropriate dimension's attribute values effectively for a specific date.

For example, a company's database may contain a table of facts that holds all the important information of the company's sales record and employees. The table would be linked to dimensions by using foreign keys. Each of these dimensions would hold various types of data such as the local offices of all the employees. However, the employees are often transferred from one office to a different one. Also, to keep track of past sales, it is necessary to report when a salesperson has been shifted to a different location.

Slowly changing dimension management is therefore required to deal with these issues, and it has various different approaches ranging from Type 0 to Type 6. Type 6 SCDs are occasionally referred to as hybrid SCDs.

Type 0
Type 0 SCD is the passive method. In this particular method, there is not really any specific action conducted, and it only manages dimensional changes, if any. Some of the dimensional values may remain the same as they were first inserted; for others, there may be new data written over the existing ones. Type 0 provides limited or no control and is not used very frequently because of the restrained potential put into resolving the dimensional issues.

Type 1
Type 1 SCD is when the change is managed by overwriting the old data and values. Type 1 SCD in data warehousing is implemented when no history is kept in the database. The current dimension data is simply overwritten by the changed one. This method of correction is

often used for the data that changes constantly with time, and it occurs by rectifying any mistakes and errors in the data (e.g., correcting misspellings, data integration, adjusting spaces). This data handling approach is simple and easy to perpetuate, but it has the disadvantage of not keeping a track of any historical data.

A Type 1 change simply overwrites the current dimensional attribute with the new information. For example, if you want to change a customer's name, the old value is discarded and the new value is reflected in the table. In this type of slowly changing dimension, no row is inserted and there is no impact on the primary key of the table. We simply update the nonprimary key columns of the table with new value.

Although 'Type 1' is a type of slowly changing dimension, we do not maintain history of change and only provide the latest data (discarding old data forever). This is useful when we don't have a requirement to maintain a history of change. An example could be data entry errors: an operator entering the wrong name of a customer in the source system (Tables 10.3 and 10.4).

In Tables 10.3 and 10.4, the state name is overwritten because the supplier would have relocated the headquarters that supplies the products.

Type 2

Type 2 SCD is when any change is reserved by using an integration of functional dates and additional rows for data storage. In this data handling approach, all of the historical dimensional changes are stored in the database. New dimensional data is constructed between the old records, and the current values are easily acquired with the history being clear. The fields "effective date" and "current indicator" are frequently used in this dimension. This method creates numerous diverse

Table 10.3 Slowly Changing Dimension Before Change in Data		
Product Name	State Name	Last Updated
Sony cyber-shot	CA	4/9/2011

Table 10.4 Slowly Changing Dimension After Change in Data		
Product Name	State Name	Last Updated
Sony cyber-shot	NY	22/01/2014

records for a given natural key in the dimension that have distinct surrogate keys, and infinite history is stored after each insert. Type 2 SCD allows us to keep a track of the historical data accurately.

Type 2 SCD creates another record and leaves the old record intact. Type 2 is the most common SCD because it allows you to track historically significant attributes. The old records point to all history before the latest change, and the new record maintains the most current information.

In this type of slowly changing dimension, we insert a new row in the table and also keep the old row. This allows business to view both rows to get a meaningful view of the change. However, data warehouse team requires design and development efforts to create the logic. Apart from development effort, this type of SCD uses additional disk space and processing power.

In this example, we initially have Table 10.5. After Rebecca moved from Kansas to New Mexico, new information was added to the table by inserting an additional row (Table 10.6).

Type 3

Type 3 SCD follows up the historical data by inserting separate individual columns for each sort of record. Customarily, in Type 3 SCD, the current and previous dimension values are kept in the database. The new value is inserted into the "current/new" column and the previous in the "old/previous" column. However, Type 3 SCD being confined to the number of columns for the deposition of history makes this technique of a limited value.

Table 10.5 Type 2 Slowly Changing Dimension Before Change in Data		
Customer Key	Name	State
1004	Rebecca	Kansas

Table 10.6 Type 2 Slowly Changing Dimension After Change in Data		
Customer Key	Name	State
1004	Rebecca	Kansas
1009	Rebecca	New Mexico

Table 10.7 Type 3 Slowly Changing Dimension Original Data Without Change		
Customer Key	Name	State
1004	Rebecca	Kansas

Table 10.8 Type 3 Slowly Changing Dimension After Change in Data				
Customer Key	Name	Original State	Current State	Effective Date
1004	Rebecca	Kansas	New Mexico	17/06/2014

Type 3 SCD should be used only if we want to maintain history in a specific manner without needing the time when change happened. Due to overhead of additional columns and lack of time window, this type of SCD is not recommended for most of business cases. We can add more columns for each change. However, this adds overhead and become useless when the number of changes per primary key goes beyond the acceptable threshold. A good example of SCD Type 3 could be a Name change database, where only the old and new names are stored.

In contrast, with Type 2 SCD, in which the history maintenance and storage are not very limited, Type 3 SCD has restricted history storage because a new column has to be inserted for each separate version, which is not very functional.

In our example, see Table 10.7. To assimilate the Type 3 SCD, we now have the additional modified and new columns shown in Table 10.8.

We have Type 1 and Type 2 SCDs as the central and overriding techniques for responding to alterations in a dimension; however, to tackle alternate realities, a third handling technique is required.

This type of slowly changing dimension is also useful for alternate reality requirements of data warehouse. For example, today we categorize a pen as a student item, but tomorrow we may also categorize it as a gift item. Now both of these categorizations are important, and we store them in this form.

Type 4

The Type 4 SCD approach is normally called using "history tables" in which a data table is used for the existing information and a subsidiary

Table 10.9 Type 4 Slowly Changing Dimension Before Change in Data		
Customer ID	**Customer Name**	**Customer Type**
1	Louis	Corporate

Table 10.10 Type 4 Slowly Changing Dimension After Change in Data				
Customer ID	**Customer Name**	**Customer Type**	**Start Date**	**End Date**
1	Louise	Retail	1/1/2010	21/07/2010
1	Louise	Management	22/07/2010	17/05/2012
1	Louise	Corporate	18/05/2012	31/12/9999

table is used for recording any alterations. The idea of Type 4 SCD is to stock up all the changes in a separate historical data record table for each separate dimension. The main dimension table holds all the current data—for example, tables for customer history (Tables 10.9 and 10.10).

Type 6

Type 6 SCD integrates the methodologies of Types 1, 2, and 3 $(1 + 2 + 3 = 6)$. In this approach, we have some additional columns in the dimension table. Particularly, Type 6 is applied if you want to maintain history completely. Additional columns are of various types, such as:

- **Current type** to maintain the current value of the attribute. For all the given items, records of history have the same existing value.
- **Historical type** is for keeping the historical value of the attribute. For a particular item of attribute, all of the history records have the same value.
- **Start date** maintains date/time when the attribute value became effective.
- **End date** maintains the date/time when the attribute value was no longer effective.
- **Current flag** maintains the value of "Y" for a record that is active or "N" for all old records.

In order to maintain history we add a new record just like SCD Type 2 and overwrite some data just like SCD Type 1, and history is maintained in another column just like SCD Type 3 (Table 10.11).

In another example, we have the supplier table initially (Table 10.12). The supplier table starts out with one record for our example supplier (Table 10.13).

When the Coca-Cola Supply Company moves to New Mexico, a new record has been added as in Type 2 processing (Table 10.14).

The current state column is overwritten with the latest value just like we do in slowly changing dimension Type 1, although old information is not lost because it is still available in other columns. To follow up with the alterations made, a new record is created as in Type 2 processing, and the history is stored in a second state column that integrates Type 3 processing (Table 10.15).

Table 10.11 Type 6 Slowly Changing Dimension Example						
Customer ID	Customer Name	Current Type	Historical Type	Start Date	End Date	Current Flag
1	Louise	A Category	C Category	1/1/2010	11/10/2015	N
2	Louise	A Category	B Category	12/10/2015	14/01/2016	N
3	Louise	A Category	A Category	15/01/2016	31/12/9999	Y

Table 10.12 Type 6 Slowly Changing Dimension Example Source Data			
Supplier Key	Supplier Code	Supplier Name	Supplier State
235	ABC	Coca-Cola	CA

Table 10.13 Type 6 Slowly Changing Dimension Example with One Record							
Supplier Key	Supplier Code	Supplier Name	Current State	Historical State	Start Data	End Date	Current Flag
235	ABC	Coca-Cola	CA	CA	2/3/2005	1/1/2005	Y

Table 10.14 Type 6 Slowly Changing Dimension Example with Two Records							
Supplier Key	Supplier Code	Supplier Name	Current State	Historical State	Start Date	End Date	Current Flag
235	ABC	Coca-Cola	IL	CA	2/3/2005	20/12/2009	N
235	ABC	Coca-Cola	IL	IL	22/12/2009	1/1/2005	Y

Table 10.16 is the supplier table as we created it earlier using the Type 6 hybrid methodology. Table 10.17 is the supplier table using the pure Type 6 methodology.

Table 10.15 Type 6 Slowly Changing Dimension Example with Three Records							
Supplier Key	Supplier Code	Supplier Name	Current State	Historical State	Start Date	End Date	Current Flag
235	ABC	Coca-Cola	NY	CA	2/3/2005	20/12/2009	N
236	ABC	Coca-Cola	NY	IL	22/12/2009	4/2/2012	N
237	ABC	Coca-Cola	NY	NY	7/2/2012	1/1/2005	Y

Table 10.16 Type 6 Slowly Changing Dimension Hybrid Example							
Supplier Key	Supplier Code	Supplier Name	Current State	Historical State	Start Date	End Date	Current Flag
235	SUP-521081	Coca-Cola	NY	CA	2/3/2005	20/12/2009	N
236	SUP-521081	Coca-Cola	NY	IL	22/12/2009	4/2/2012	N
237	SUP-521081	Coca-Cola	NY	NY	7/2/2012	1/1/2005	Y

Table 10.17 Pure Type 6 Slowly Changing Dimension Example					
Supplier Key	Supplier Code	Supplier Name	Supplier State	Start Date	End Date
456	SUP-521081	Coca-Cola	CA	2/3/2005	20/12/2009
456	SUP-521081	Coca-Cola	IL	22/12/2009	4/2/2012
456	SUP-521081	Coca-Cola	NY	7/2/2012	1/1/2005

Temporal Database

Some applications need to design and build databases in which information changes over time. Doing so without a temporal table support is possible but complex.

Consider an application for an insurance company that uses a policy table in which the definition looks like this:

```
CREATE TABLE POLICY(
POLICY_ID INTEGER,
CUSTOMER_ID INTEGER,
POLICY_TYPE CHAR(2),
POLICY_DETAILS CHAR(40)
)
UNIQUE PRIMARY INDEX(POLICY_ID);
```

Suppose the application needs to record when rows in the policy table became valid. Without temporal table support, one approach that the application can take is to add a DATE column to the policy table called Start_Date. Suppose the application also needs to know when rows in the table are no longer valid. Another DATE column called End_Date can accomplish this.

The new definition of the table looks like this:

```
CREATE TABLE POLICY(
POLICY_ID INTEGER,
CUSTOMER_ID INTEGER,
POLICY_TYPE CHAR(2),
POLICY_DETAILS CHAR(40)
START_DATE DATE,
END_DATE DATE
)
UNIQUE PRIMARY INDEX(POLICY_ID);
```

Several complications are now evident. For example, if a customer makes a change to his or her policy during the life of the policy, a new row will need to be created to store the new policy conditions that are in effect from that time until the end of the policy. But the policy conditions before the change are also likely to be important to retain for historical reasons. The original row represents the conditions that were in effect for the beginning portion of the policy, but the END_DATE will need to be updated to reflect when the policy conditions were changed.

Additionally, because of these types of changes, it becomes likely that more than one row will now have the same value for Policy_ID, so the primary index for the table would need to change. All modifications to the table must now consider changing the Start_Date and End_Date columns. Queries will be more complicated.

The mere presence of a DATE column in a table does not make the table a temporal table, and it does not make the database a temporal database. A temporal database must record the time-varying nature of the information managed by the enterprise.

Rather than using approaches such as adding DATE columns to traditional tables, a temporal database provides support to effectively create, query, and modify time-varying tables in a completely different manner.

There are two types of times in the context of temporal databases.

Transaction Time
Definition
Transaction time deals with the time when a certain fact was stored or deleted from the database. Transaction time is mostly used for traceability or auditability purposes and will almost always be present in regulatory scenarios.

Limitations
• Supplied and maintained by the DBMS
• Query semantics for asking questions about when the database "knew" the fact
• Can only be one per table
• Always defined as NOT NULL Timestamp(6) with time zone
• Maintained automatically unless nontemporal capabilities are granted

Valid Time
Definition
Valid time denotes the time period during which a fact is true with respect to the real world (e.g., on January 1, 2010, John Smith's bank account balance was $10,000). Valid time is maintained by the system but can be changed by the user. Valid time is the start time and end time of a period during which a fact was true.

Limitations
• Supplied by the user or application
• Maintained by the database
• Query semantics for asking questions about when the fact was valid per the organization's definitions
• Can be maintained by the application and the system
• Can only be one per table
• Can be defined as date, time, or timestamp
• Can be NULL or NOT NULL (whole column, meaning both begin and end)

History Data Verification
If the source claims that it maintains the history of the data, then the data mapper must confirm that the time window in the source is defined correctly and that it can be imported to the data warehouse as

is. If there are issues in the source data, then data warehouse needs to re-create history or mark the table as a nonhistory table.

Below are some scenarios that must be tested on source data for history handling verification.

-- Scenario #1: CHECKING FOR NULL IN START/END DATE COLUMN
-- This test will identify the record(s), having NULLs in Start_Date column.

```
SELECT
'HHI NULL'
,'EMPLOYEE_ADDRESS'
,a.Employee_Id
-- ,a.Address_Id
,a.Employee_Address_Role_Cd
-- ,a.Employee_Address_Start_Dt
,a.start_date
,a.end_Date
FROM
DW.dbo.Employee_Address a
WHERE
a.start_date IS NULL
GROUP BY 1,2, 3, 4, 5, 6 ;
```

-- Scenario #2: CHECKING FOR REVERSE CASE
-- This test will identify the record(s), having Start_Date of the record greater than the End_Date.
-- End_Date_n < Start_Date_n

```
SELECT
'HHI REVERSE'
, 'EMPLOYEE_ADDRESS'
,a.Employee_Id
-- ,a.Address_Id
,a.Employee_Address_Role_Cd
-- ,a.Employee_Address_Start_Dt
,a.start_date
,a.end_Date
FROM
DW.dbo.Employee_Address a
WHERE
a.start_date > a.end_Date
GROUP BY 1,2, 3, 4, 5, 6 ;
```

-- Scenario #3: CHECKING RECORDS WITH HISTORY OVERLAPS/COLLISION
-- This test will bring records with overlapping or collision in history periods.
-- Collision: End_Date_n = Start_Date_n+1
-- Overlap: End_Date_n > Start_Date_n+1

```
SELECT
'HHI OVERLAP'
, 'EMPLOYEE_ADDRESS'
,a.Employee_Id
-- ,a.Address_Id
,a.Employee_Address_Role_Cd
-- ,a.Employee_Address_Start_Dt
, a.start_date
, a.end_Date as a_End_Date
, b.start_date
, b.end_Date as b_End_Date
FROM
DW.dbo.Employee_Address a
INNER JOIN
DW.dbo.Employee_Address b
ON
a.Employee_Id = b.Employee_Id
--and a.Address_Id = b.Address_Id
and
a.Employee_Address_Role_Cd = b.Employee_Address_Role_Cd
--and a.Employee_Address_Start_Dt = b.Employee_Address_Start_Dt
WHERE
(
(
  a.start_date < b.start_date
  AND
  a_End_Date >= b_End_Date
)
OR
(
  a.start_date <= b.start_date
  AND
  a_End_Date > b.start_date
  AND
  a_End_Date < b_End_Date
)
OR
(
  a_End_Date > b.start_date
  AND
```

```
    a.start_date < b.start_date
    AND
    b_End_Date IS NULL
  )
  )
AND
(
a_End_Date NOT = b.start_date
) ;
```

-- Scenario #4: CHECKING RECORDS WITH GAP
-- According to the history handling rules, there should not be gaps in the history period.
-- That is, when a record is closed, the next record should be active, starting right at the time and date the previous record was closed.
-- Gap: End_Date_n < Start_Date_n+1 − 1

```
SELECT
'HHI GAPS'
, 'EMPLOYEE_ADDRESS'
,a.Employee_Id
-- ,a.Address_Id
,a.Employee_Address_Role_Cd
-- ,a.Employee_Address_Start_Dt
, a.start_date AS a_from
, a.end_Date AS a_to
, MIN(b.start_date) AS b_from
, MIN(b.end_Date) AS b_to
FROM
DW.dbo.Employee_Address a
INNER JOIN
DW.dbo.Employee_Address b
ON
a.Employee_Id = b.Employee_Id
--and a.Address_Id = b.Address_Id
  and
a.Employee_Address_Role_Cd = b.Employee_Address_Role_Cd
--and a.Employee_Address_Start_Dt = b.Employee_Address_Start_Dt
AND
a.end_Date < b.start_date
GROUP BY
1, 2, 3, 4, 5, 6
HAVING
a_to <> (b_from - 1) ;
```

-- Scenario #5: CHECKING MULTIPLE OPEN RECORDS
-- According to the history handling rules, there should not be two open records at the same time.
-- That is, two records with same Pk_Id and different Start_Dates but both records have End_Dates as nulls.

```
SELECT
'MULTIPLE OPEN RECORDS'
,a.Employee_Id
-- ,a.Address_Id
,a.Employee_Address_Role_Cd
-- ,a.Employee_Address_Start_Dt
,a.end_Date
FROM
DW.dbo.Employee_Address a
WHERE
a.end_Date IS NULL
GROUP BY
1,2, 3, 4
HAVING COUNT(*) > 1 ;
```

SQL TOOLS

SQL is the best tool for data mappers. It is important that data mappers can write the right and effective SQL code for data analysis. There are some tricks that help automate data analysis and turn data analysis into a well-defined process. Below we discuss some features of SQL that data mappers should use for analysis.

Automatic Query Generators

Writing an analysis query for every table and column of the source requires lot of time and coding effort. To make the process faster and more accurate, we can use SQL to generate SQL.

Almost all database systems store metadata about tables and columns. We can use this metadata to generate generic queries for data analysis.

If we are looking for table-level analysis, we can check whether a table has full row duplicates or not. The query below will generate SQL statements for all tables of the database.

```
SELECT 'SELECT'
UNION
SELECT
  Column_Name
  +','
FROM dbo.informationSchemaColumns
WHERE Database_Name = 'any source db'
UNION
SELECT 'Count (*) FROM ' + TABLENAME
  + ' GROUP BY ' FROM dbo.informationSchemaTables
WHERE Database_Name = 'any source db'
UNION
SELECT
  Column_Name
  +','
FROM dbo.informationSchemaColumns
WHERE Database_Name = 'any source db'
UNION
SELECT 'HAVING COUNT (*) > 1 ;'
```

The above query will generate SQL code for every table but will not run as it is. You need to modify some parts of the code. In some cases, the result may be unsorted, resulting in wrong or unreadable code. For this, you can add an integer value in each select statement above in sequence (or use column sequence numbers in metadata) and sort the resultset. This will ensure that a single query is in the same place and in the correct sequence.

The idea here is to reduce the effort of analyzing every table. This query can be further improved by adding checks for the last column, first column, sorting, and so on. This one-time effort will help the data mapper in the long run because this generator can be reused in other projects.

Similar to tables, we also do analysis of columns to identify different aspects.

Aggregate Functions

Sometimes we need aggregate functions for data analysis. These functions can be used for verifying individual column values or for comparing source data with another system to confirm aggregated values.

Different database systems have different aggregate functions, but all provide basic ones. Below are the ones that are most commonly used during data analysis.

COUNT: This function counts the number of occurrences of a column(s).
SUM: This function adds all values of the column.
MIN: This function returns minimum value from the column.
MAX: This function returns maximum value from the column.

These functions are usually used with other SQL features to get the desired resultset. For example, if you want to see how much sales volume was generated for a certain type of product, then you can use a CASE statement with the SUM function:

```
SUM
    (
       CASE WHEN Product_Type = 1 THEN Aount ELSE 0 END
    )
```

COUNT(*) gives a count of all rows in a table, we can add DISTINCT on column to get count of unique values of the column COUNT (DISTINCT employee_id)

Window and Rank Functions

A window function performs a calculation across a set of table rows that are somehow related to the current row. This is comparable to the type of calculation that can be done with an aggregate function. But unlike regular aggregate functions, use of a window function does not cause rows to become grouped into a single output row; instead, the rows retain their separate identities. Behind the scenes, the window function is able to access more than just the current row of the query result.

In the code example below, we are comparing the salary of a single employee with his department's average.

```
SELECT depname, empno, salary
, avg(salary) OVER (PARTITION BY depname)
FROM empsalary;
```

In the code sample below, we are ranking each employee based on his/her salary within his/her department. The partition clause allows us to define the area within which ranking is done and order by clause is used to define ranking criteria.

```
SELECT department, employee, monthly_Income, rank() OVER (PARTITION
BY department ORDER BY monthly_Income DESC) FROM Employee_Salary;
```

We can also define the window in which a function is applied. In the following code example we are aggregating all data before the current value.

```
SELECT Week_Number,
SUM() over
(ORDER BY Week_Number ROWS
        between unbounded preceding
            and current row
) As Running_Sum
FROM Monthly_Sales;
```

MICROSOFT EXCEL AND OTHER TOOLS

SQL is an excellent tool for data analysis, but sometimes it is easier to do multiple actions on small datasets in a Microsoft Excel file rather than running queries again and again on the database server. The case for Excel is stronger when the database server is slow and takes time in running the simple queries.

Using such tools helps data mappers get results quickly and uses most of the time on devising a strategy for analysis. Below we will explain some of the features that are commonly used during the data mapping process.

Remove Duplicates

Removing duplicates from data in SQL requires a GROUP BY or DISTINCT function, but we might run a new query every time we have a different combination of columns. Instead, we can export the complete dataset to an Excel file and use Excel's "Remove Duplicate" function for this purpose (Figure 10.1).

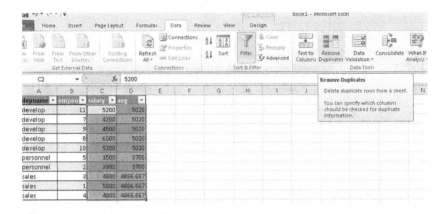

Figure 10.1 Example of removing duplicates.

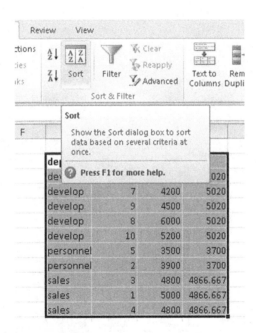

Figure 10.2 Example of sorting data.

Sort

By sorting data in different orders using different columns, Excel can reduce the query execution time on the database server. The concept is similar to the SQL ORDER BY clause (Figure 10.2).

We can sort on multiple columns and on different options (Figure 10.3).

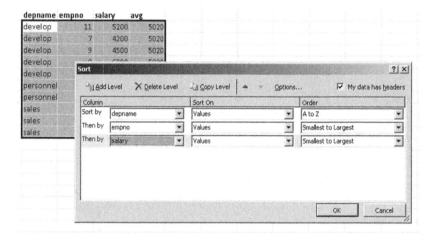

Figure 10.3 Sorting data options available in Excel.

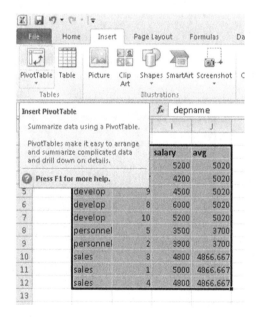

Figure 10.4 Creating a pivot table in Excel.

Pivot Tables

The best feature Excel provides to a data mapper is pivot tables, which can be used to see the final reports from a business user's perspective within seconds. Pivot tables in Excel provide a drag-and-drop option to view aggregated data using different combinations of columns (Figure 10.4).

Figure 10.5 Selecting columns as measures and dimensions in Excel.

Sum of salary	Column Labels			
Row Labels	develop	personnel	sales	Grand Total
1			5000	5000
2		3900		3900
3			4800	4800
4			4800	4800
5		3500		3500
7	4200			4200
8	6000			6000
9	4500			4500
10	5200			5200
11	5200			5200
Grand Total	25100	7400	14600	47100

Figure 10.6 Pivot table result in Excel.

You can select any column for dimension and measure (Figure 10.5). The result is displayed in a pivot table immediately (Figure 10.6).

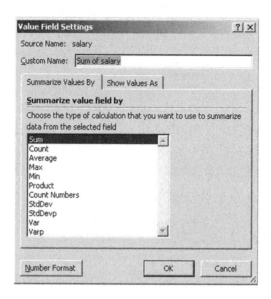

Figure 10.7 Measure (calculated column) options in Excel.

There are many options available for the measure part of the pivot table, and the data mapper can select options based on specific requirements (Figure 10.7).

CHAPTER 11

Data Quality

Data warehousing is gaining in eminence as organizations become aware of the benefits of decision-oriented and business astuteness–oriented databases. However, there is one key stumbling block to the rapid development and implementation of quality data warehouses—that of warehouse data quality issues at sundry stages of data warehousing. Specifically, quandaries arise in populating a warehouse with quality data.

The end purpose of data warehouse is to provide business users with a tool to make decisions. If the information in these reports is incorrect, then actions taken by end users might be damaging for business (Figure 11.1).

The cost of re-doing data warehouse design and development to fix data quality issues can be the deal breaker, where organizations lose interest in such systems. Even if we identify data quality issues at a later stage of the data warehouse life cycle, the fixes usually are done for a particular issue and do not address all aspects of data quality.

The underlying issues in source data result in the success or failure of data warehouse. Since source systems have been storing data for pre-data warehouse time, it is not possible to fix issues in the source system. It is therefore ownership of data warehouse to identify and fix all data quality issues.

Quality of data is directly dependant on the number of source systems and their geographical distribution. Loading data from a single location will result in fewer data quality issues; however, if the source is running in different countries, the number of data quality issues will be higher. Consider a mobile company's warranty claim data: people entering data into the system can be working anywhere in the world. In some places the operator might not pay attention to entering correct data into the system, as his or her focus would be to fix the device. When such data is loaded in to the data warehouse, getting a single picture of all data becomes very difficult due to data quality issues, and it is almost impossible to get value out of the data warehouse.

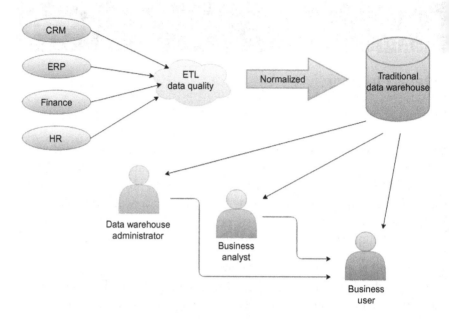

Figure 11.1 Interaction with data warehouse and users. CRM, customer relationship management; ERP, enterprise resource planning; ETL, extract, transform, load; HR, human resources.

Before the computer industry produced inexpensive machines, government agencies maintained address information using mainframes. The business rules were applied to fix misspellings and typographical data quality issues.

This data was shared among selected services organizations, and an updated version was maintained. This resulted in fewer data quality errors, and anyone accessing this data could use it without worry.

WHAT IS DATA QUALITY?

Data quality can be defined as issues in source data that reduce the chances of producing correct business reports for end users. Data quality is about having confidence in the quality of the data that you record and the data that you use. Data can take many forms and types such as numbers, symbols, words, images, and graphics that, once processed, become useful information (Figure 11.3).

For example, in the health care field, safe, reliable health care depends on access to and utilization of quality data. A user's personal

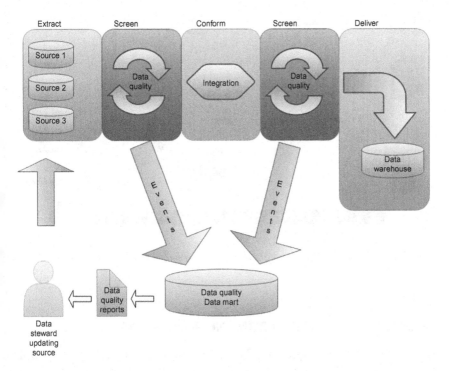

Figure 11.2 Data quality integration in the data life cycle.

health care data apprises all aspects of his or her care, including refer-ral, assessment, investigations, diagnosis, treatment or care plans, and follow-up. Correct and up-to-date data is critical, not only for the pro-vision of high-quality clinical services but also for perpetuating care, research, strategic orchestrating, and management of health and long term care accommodations.

If the data is of poor quality overall, it results in a difference in the end reports, leading to a lack of confidence in using it. This means that opportunities to ameliorate the quality of the data will be disor-iented, ultimately undermining opportunities for accommodation amendment. Driving amelioration in your data quality will ultimately avail you and your colleagues to provide a better accommodation (Figure 11.2).

When the correct data is available in a timely manner to decision makers who can confidently rely on it, the data is considered quality data.

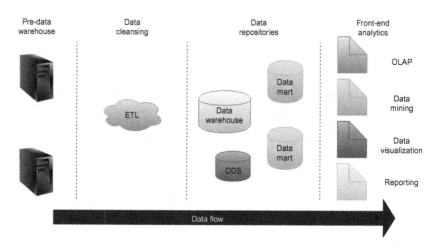

Figure 11.3 Data flow and transformation. ETL, extract, transform, load; ODS, Operational Data Source; OLAP, Online Analytical Processing.

HOW DO YOU BENEFIT FROM DATA QUALITY?

Let's take the example of the health care sector, where people distributing health care need access to quality data in order to perform their duties. The benefits of accumulating and using quality data include:

1. Supporting you and your colleagues to distribute safe, high-quality care to users
2. Providing a precise picture of care and good documentary evidence of your work
3. Helping in the coordination of care with your colleagues
4. Ensuring you meet licit requisites such as those under the Data Auspice Acts
5. Ensuring you meet professional standards
6. Supporting the provision of data for clinical and audit initiatives
7. Supporting decision making within your organization and nationally
8. Providing data for health care research, which may lead to improved outcomes for your users or better ways of working for you

It is paramount to understand that poor data quality has a substantial impact on the safety of users. Therefore, data quality is the responsibility of all staff (Figure 11.4).

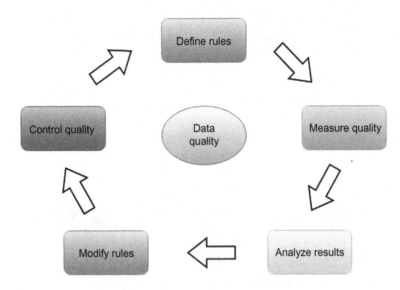

Figure 11.4 The data quality life cycle.

FACTORS DETERMINING DATA QUALITY

Loading source data and making reports do not mean that business users can always make decisions and perform actions smoothly. Dealing with missing data, data with errors, or data that is out of context is another definition of data quality. A broader definition is that data quality is achieved when an organization uses data that is comprehensive, understandable, consistent, pertinent, and timely.

The first step toward data quality improvement is to understand the dimensions of data quality. Source data has to meet criteria of data quality to ensure that it is effective and interpretable. In other words, we can define high-quality data can be defined as data that satisfy all dimensions of data quality.

Many definitions are available for data quality, and there has been considerable effort made to identify its dimensions. The main point when defining the dimensions of data quality is to keep in mind that high-quality data should be available to business users for making decisions.

Below we discuss globally acceptable dimensions of data related to data warehousing (Figure 11.5).

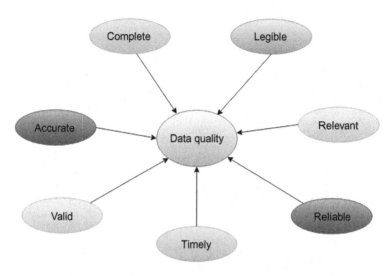

Figure 11.5 Factors determining data quality.

Accurate Data

Data that uniquely defines its logical concept along with detailed data can be defined as accurate data.

Examples include:

- Identification details are correct and uniquely identify the service user. For example, the address on the record is correct.
- All pages in the health or social care record are for the same person.
- The vital signs are correctly transcribed from the measurement monitor to the health care record.
- The abstracted data for statistics and registries meets relevant standards and has been verified for accuracy.
- When predetermined coding standards exist, it is vital that all codes used conform to these standards.
- Each data field is defined so that it is clear what type of data is to be recorded in a particular field. For example, date of birth is in the format dd/mm/yyyy (e.g., 22/10/2012).

Complete Data

Complete data has the those items required to measure the intended activity or event.

Examples include:

- All interactions with a service are documented fully in the health or social care record.
- Abbreviations should be avoided if possible and only used when approved by the organization.
- Vague phrases such as "usual day" and relative expressions such as "improved" are avoided.
- The prescription and dispensing sections of the health or social care record include the name of any prescribed drug printed with the dosage, route, and time of administration clearly documented.
- International units of measurement are clearly documented on all laboratory results.

Legible Data

Legible data is data that the intended users will find easy to read and understand.

Examples include:

- Care is taken to ensure that handwritten documents such as prescriptions, discharge summaries, care center daily logs, and transfer or referral letters use text that is clear and readable.
- Handwritten notes are completed in permanent ink and are clear, concise, and easy to read and understand.
- In all health and social care records, both manual and electronic, only codes, symbols, or abbreviations approved by the organization are used.

Relevant Data

Relevant data meets the needs of the information users.

Examples include:

- A current contact telephone number and address are provided to the public health nurse when a mother and baby are discharged from a maternity hospital or maternity unit.
- Foster care records include whether the children are in voluntary care or statutory care, so that consent can be obtained from the appropriate person for issues such as receiving vaccinations.

- The discharge summary from a hospital to a family doctor contains all relevant information, such as diagnoses and procedures carried out, to ensure continuity of care.
- A referral letter from a family doctor to a hospital specialist contains the data required for the referral to be appropriately assessed and processed.

Reliable Data

Reliable data is collected consistently over time and reflects the true facts.

Examples include:
- Data such as date of birth are recorded on the first sheet and all subsequent sheets of the health care record.
- The correct name and hospital number of the individual is recorded on all paper forms within the health care record at the point of care or service.
- Aftercare plans for children in foster care approaching 18 years of age are completed consistently for all children.

Timely Data

In today's changing world, getting information at the right time is crucial in making timely decisions. For some organizations, data warehouse is a tool to predict future patterns, and if we cannot provide information at the right time, then business decisions can be wrong.

Examples include:
- An individual's identifying information is recorded at the time of first attendance and is readily available to identify the individual at any given time during his or her care and treatment.
- For hospital patients, all interactions are documented at the point of care or as soon as possible afterward.
- On discharge or the death of a patient in hospital, his or her health care records are processed and completed within a specified time frame.
- Reports and data for national registries and databases are validated and are available within a specified time frame.
- The end-of-life preferences of residents in nursing homes are clearly documented and available when urgent decisions are required in relation to end-of-life care.

Valid Data

Data that is needed for its intended purpose is valid data. It is loaded from the source and is measured on correct and meaningful parameters.

Examples include:

- Unique numbers that are used to identify the service user are validated to ensure the correct number is assigned to the correct service user.
- For hospital patients, the date of admission to the hospital must be the same as or earlier than the date of discharge from the facility.
- For hospital patients, validity checks are carried out on vital statistics recorded such as body temperature and blood pressure to ensure that they fall within valid ranges.

STAGES OF DATA WAREHOUSING SUSCEPTIBLE TO DATA QUALITY PROBLEMS

In this section we will list stages of the data warehouse life cycle, where we encounter data quality issues.

- Source system
- Analysis and profiling stage
- Data extraction from the source, loading in staging and during transformation
- Designing the database

Data quality issues can arise during maintenance, insertion, processing, extraction, transformation, receiving, and loading. There are many processes that bring data into the data warehouse; some of these have an impact on the quality of data. While we identify and rectify most of data quality issues, some of them will still exist. Such scenarios should be reported to the business users so that actions can be taken if it is not acceptable. For example, if the source system does not provide the bank account number of a financial transaction, there is nothing that data warehouse can do to fix this. Client should have a clear understanding of such issues.

There are many ways we can face data quality problems. Below are some common ones:

- Processes for handling data in source
- Processes that govern data entry and their implementation
- Migration errors when loading data from one system to another
- Data that is not in control of client—i.e., third-party data

The main point here is that we can face quality issues at any stage of data flow from source system to business reports. Figure 11.6 shows data warehouse stages where data quality issues can arise.

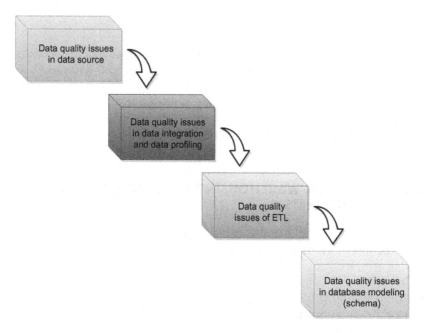

Figure 11.6 Stages of data warehousing susceptible to data quality problems.

CLASSIFICATION OF DATA QUALITY ISSUES

Data analysts identify the root cause of data quality issues and make design decisions to address such problems. In this section we will identify areas on which analysts need to focus.

Data Quality Issues at Data Sources

A leading cause of data warehousing and business intelligence project failure is erroneous or poor quality source data. Eventually, data in the data warehouse is collected from various sources as depicted later. The source system consists of all of those "transaction/production" raw data providers from which the details are pulled to make it useful for data warehousing. All of these source systems have their own methods of storing data. Some of the data sources are cooperative, and some are uncooperative. Because of this diversity, several reasons are present that may contribute to data quality problems if they are not taken care of. A source that offers any kind of unsecured access can become unreliable, ultimately contributing to poor data quality.

Table 11.1 Causes of Data Quality Problems in Source Systems
Data source inclusion that have no value for business
The closer we get to source for extraction, the more data quality issues increase
Lack of information about intra-source system connection
An inability to cope with aging data
Varying timeliness of data sources
Lack of validation routines at sources
Unexpected changes in source systems
Multiple data sources generating semantic heterogeneity
Use of different representation formats in data sources
The presence of duplicate records of the same data in multiple sources

Data sources can have many issues associated with data quality. For example, legacy data sources do not maintain metadata to describe them. Sources also receive data from different channels—i.e., human data entry, manual files, or through another database. Since the requirement in sources is to track a transaction/event, data quality is acceptable for them as it does not impact business. However, when this data is loaded to a data warehouse, we need to identify and fix such issues.

Another example is file-based sources where multiple files are combined to generate a single file, resulting in data quality issues. Table 11.1 summarizes the possible causes of data quality issues at the source stage of data warehousing (Figure 11.7).

Data Quality Issues During the Data Profiling Stage

When possible candidate data sources are identified and finalized, data profiling comes into play immediately. Data profiling is the examination and assessment of the source systems' data quality, integrity, and consistency, sometimes additionally called *source systems analysis*. Data profiling is fundamental yet is often ignored or given less attention; as result, the quality of the data in the warehouse is compromised. At the commencement of a data warehouse project, as soon as a candidate data source is identified, data profiling assessment should be made to provide a "go" or "no-go" decision about proceeding with the project. Table 11.2 depicts the possible causes of data quality degradation at the data profiling stage of data warehousing.

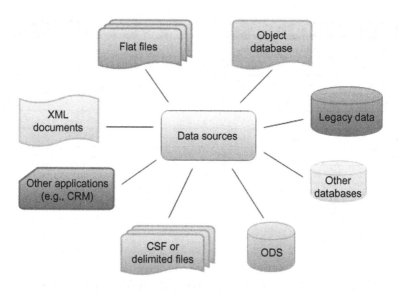

Figure 11.7 Data quality problems in the source system. CSF, Comma Separated Values; ODS, Operational Data Source.

Table 11.2 Data Quality Issues During the Data Profiling Stage
Insufficient data profiling of data sources
Manually derived information about the data contents in operational systems
Inappropriate selection of the automated profiling tool
Insufficient data content analysis against external reference data
Lack of analysis of source data structures
Lack of analysis of fields in each source system's table
Lack of source system's inter-table relationships
Lack of data available for analysis to get full picture
Lack of analysis of aggregated data on source system
Lack of documentation during profiling stage

Data Quality Issues During the Extract, Transform, Load Phase

Data cleansing is required when data is extracted from the source system, loaded into staging tables or transformed to the target data warehouse area. These improvements are usually executed to improve precision of the data warehouse.

Once data is extracted from the source system, further data quality improvements are done in the staging area. This area, along with ETL

Table 11.3 Data Quality Issues During the Extract, Transform, Load Stage
Misinterpreting or wrong implementation of the SCD strategy in the ETL phase
Type of staging area (relational or nonrelational)
Different business rules of various data sources
Business rules lacking currency
The inability to schedule extracts by time, interval, or event
No analysis of source system's changes
Multiple extracts in staging area or other data refresh issues
Staging area's permanent deletion of data
Removing referential integrity constraints in staging area
Lack of reflection of rules established for data cleaning into the metadata
ETL, extract, transform, load; SCD, slowly changing dimension.

(Extract, Transform, Load), are most critical stages of a data warehouse and the data mapper's maximum focus should be to fix all data quality issues here. This stage is perfect for identifying issues and tracking them. Some reasons for data quality issues during this phase are listed in Table 11.3.

Data Quality Issues During Data Modeling

Usefulness of reporting information is the main goal of a data warehouse team. Below are three things that impact information:

- Overall data quality
- Applications that are running the data warehouse
- Data model quality

Special attention should be give to the data model of the warehouse as data will be stored in it. Any issue with the design will have a huge impact on final reporting. Some of the issues are gradually transmuting dimensions, rapidly transmuting dimensions, and multivalued dimensions.

A flawed schema impacts negatively on information quality. Table 11.4 depicts some of the most consequential causes of data quality issues during the data warehouse schema designing stage.

Table 11.4 Data Quality Issues in Schema Design
Incomplete or wrong requirement analysis of the project, leading to poor schema design
Lack of currency in business rules, causing poor requirement analysis, leading to poor schema design
Choice of the dimensional modeling (STAR, SNOWFLAKE, FACT CONSTELLATION) schema
Late identification of SCDs
Late-arriving dimensions
Improper selection of record granularity, leading to poor schema design
Wrong primary keys of facts or dimension tables
Inability to support database schema refactoring
Multivalued dimensions
Lack of sufficient validation and integrity rules in the schema
SCD, slowly changing dimension.

HOW CAN YOU ASSESS DATA QUALITY?

To improve data quality, you first need to quantify the data quality to identify what needs to be amended. Efforts to improve systems or processes must be driven by reliable data that not only sanctions deficiencies to be accurately identified but also prioritizes quality amelioration initiatives and enables objective assessment of whether change and amelioration have occurred. Organizations should have a dedicated staff member who assesses the overall data quality on a customary substructure.

Assessing data quality will allow you to:

- Establish a baseline for data quality and identify any areas for amelioration.
- Demonstrate which areas have been amended or improved.
- Assess the impact of any transmutations in practice, policies, or procedures on data quality.
- Improve confidence in the data.

The simplest way to assess data quality is to review a representative sample of data to ensure that:

- It has been recorded in keeping with policies and procedures.
- Mandatory values in a dataset have been included.
- It is within acceptable ranges (if quantitative).
- It adheres to the seven data quality dimensions as outlined in this chapter.

When developing a data quality assessment plan, certain initial steps should be taken, which include:

- Assigning responsibility: A categorical staff member should be assigned to audit aspects of data contained in the service records
- Identifying how you might measure paramount aspects of data quality such as precision, completeness, legibility, relevance or pertinence, reliability, timeliness, and validity
- Determining indicators of data quality for each data item (e.g., the percentage of the completeness of the vocation field in service records)
- Identifying the most appropriate or congruous method for quantifying the indicators (e.g., by user questionnaire or by statistical analysis of the data)
- Using the developed indicators or designators of data quality to engender an organized method for collecting and reviewing data.

After the initial steps are taken, the findings of data quality assessments should be shared with all appropriate staff, including senior management and all those involved in the amassment of data. Any needed actions to improve the data quality should be identified.

WHAT CAN YOU DO TO MAKE DATA QUALITY A SUCCESS?

The collection and use of quality data by staff is an integral part of practice to ensure safe and effective service delivery to the customer. Staff members have a professional obligation to maintain documentation that is clear, concise, and comprehensive and to keep an accurate and true record of service. The same principles should apply to all other staff recording data in electronic or paper formats.

When you are recording data, it should:

- Be a clear, concise, factual, full record of service.
- Comply with data definitions when these exist and only use approved abbreviations.
- Be legible, sempiternal, service user focused, and nonjudgmental.
- Include the date and time of service or event (including recording changes or addendums).
- Avoid duplication of data that already exists.

- Be timely and complete as near as possible to the episode of service or event.
- Identify the details of the person who provided the service and the person who documented the accommodation or event.
- Minimize transcription of data.

You are personally accountable and responsible for the data that you record, and you can have a direct effect on data quality.

CHAPTER 12

Data Mapping Scenarios

So far we have discussed data mapping prerequisites, general definitions, and formats. In this chapter, we will discuss in detail different mapping scenarios and provide different options available to data mappers. We will discuss the best possible solution to the problem and create a mapping from the source to the target. In each scenario, we will provide sample data, a logical data model (LDM) table, and other details required for the mapping.

DATA TRANSFORMATION (NORMALIZED MODEL)

Let's start with an example that covers most of the basic transformations.

Source

There are three sources in this example, all providing data for the party target table.

The first source is the Employee_Detail table from the human resources (HR) source system. The second source is the Monthly_Salary table from the finance source system containing employee salary information for every month. The third is the customer table from the sales department's database. This table contains information about the customers to which the company provides services and products.

Because in LDM we generalize, we store all kind of parties in the PARTY table. The first two sources provide data for the same party (i.e., employee), and the third source provides data for customers.

Target

In this example, the target table is party (Figure 12.1).

PARTY

Party_Id Party_Type
Party_First_Name Party_Last_Name Party_Desc Party_Date_Of_Birth Party_Start _Dttm Party_Subtype_Cd Party_Department

Figure 12.1 Target table for the data transformation scenario.

Although we don't have the actual start date of an employee, we do have the salary date. This is the best we can do with the available data.

Mapping

Because there are multiple sources for this table, we have to assign priority to each mapping. The priority can be defined and implemented in multiple ways. We will use a simple method for defining priority whereby a numeric value will be multiplied by another value known as a multiplier value, which will separate for each mapping. This method requires a metadata table in which we will store target table name, source table ID (which is unique for each table in the Enterprise Data Warehouse [EDW]), record ID, and a multiplier value. Later on, this metadata table will be used in the extract, transform, load (ETL) process when applying data from the load-ready area to the target EDW table.

The priority of each mapping is defined based on input received from the source, data analysis carried out, and input received from the subject matter expert (SME).

In this particular example, HR data is being used. The client information technology (IT) team has stated that this data will contain values for almost all columns, finance and sales data, and some information about party. In this example, the multiplier value for the HR source table is taken as 100; for the finance table, it is 90; and for the sales table, it is 100. Note that HR and finance are providing data for the same party, but sales is providing data for a logically different party. The primary key of the table contains a Party_Type column, which helps in distinguishing employees from customers and other types of parties.

It is possible that in the future, a new source might provide better data than finance but not as complete as HR. In that case, a multiplier value of 95 can be assigned to that source table. Thus, it can be seen that the range of values used for the source table multiplier is such that it provides flexibility for inclusion of future sources in the priority list for the party table.

For better readability of the mapping (Table 12.1), only important columns of the mapping have been used.

We have defined priority of the mapping in the header rule area along with table-level rules. Note that we have also populated an indicator in the header row, giving information about the master or secondary source. A plus sign represents the master source for this information, and a minus sign represents sources that don't provide complete data for logical entity. This information helps future SMEs to change priority or importance of the data from a source.

DATA JOINING (NORMALIZED MODEL)

Data joining between source tables creates complexity in data mappings. The main idea is to use data from different tables and store it in one target table. This is necessary when:

1. Source tables have mutually exclusive information.
2. A lookup is required in another table to get information.
3. The target table is denormalized.
4. Data quality improvement is required by using another table's data.
5. Lookup in the target table is required.
6. The surrogate key lookup is required.

Data joining should be explained in detail, giving information about columns to join on, type of join (e.g., left, inner), missing data conditions, and data loading time.

If two staging tables are joined, then they must be in synchronization with respect to the source (i.e., at the time of mapping execution, both tables should have the required information). The rules must also consider delayed loading (e.g., if data loading is done for four extracts, then what rule will be applied if there will be duplicates in joining tables?).

Table 12.1 Data Mapping for the Data Transformation Scenario

Target Table	Target Column	Record Id	Source Table	Source Column	TRN CAT*	Transformation Rule
Party		HRD001	Employee_Detail		+	P = 100 If there are multiple rows for one Employee_Id then select latest based on extract timestamp
Party	Party_Id	HRD001	Employee_Detail	Employee_Id	Direct	
Party	Party_Type	HRD001	CONSTANT	"1"	Hardcode	"1 for "Employee"
Party	Party_First_Name	HRD001	Employee_Detail	Given_Name	Direct	
Party	Party_Last_Name	HRD001	Employee_Detail	Family_Name	Direct	
Party	Party_Desc	HRD001	Employee_Detail	Nick_Name	Direct	
Party	Party_Date_Of_Birth	HRD001	Employee_Detail	DOB	Direct	
Party	Party_Start_Dttm	HRD001	Employee_Detail	Joining_Date	Direct	
Party	Party_Subtype	HRD001	CONSTANT	"1"	Hardcode	"1 for "INDIVIDUAL"
Party	Party_Department	HRD001	Employee_Detail	Department_Id	Direct	
Party		FIN001	Monthly_Salary		−	P = 90 If there are multiple rows for one Employee_Id then select latest based on extract timestamp
Party	Party_Id	FIN001	Monthly_Salary	Employee_Id	Direct	
Party	Party_Type	FIN001	CONSTANT	"1"	Hardcode	"1 for "Employee"
Party	Party_First_Name	FIN001	Monthly_Salary	First_Name	Direct	
Party	Party_Last_Name	FIN001	Monthly_Salary	Family_Name	Direct	
Party	Party_Desc	FIN001	CONSTANT	NULL	Hardcode	

Entity	Target Column	Source Table	Source Type	Source Column	TRN CAT*	Comment
Party	Party_Date_Of_Birth	FIN001	CONSTANT	NULL	Hardcode	
Party	Party_Start_Dttm	FIN001	Monthly_Salary	Salary_Date	Direct	
Party	Party_Subtype	FIN001	CONSTANT	"1"	Hardcode	"1 for "INDIVIDUAL"
Party	Party_Department	FIN001	CONSTANT	NULL	Hardcode	
Party		FIN001	Customer		+	P = 100. If there are multiple rows for one Customer_Id then select latest based on extract timestamp
Party	Party_Id	FIN001	Customer	Customer_Id	Direct	
Party	Party_Type	FIN001	CONSTANT	"2"	Hardcode	"2 for "Customer"
Party	Party_First_Name	FIN001	Customer	Customer_Name	Direct	
Party	Party_Last_Name	FIN001	CONSTANT	NULL	Hardcode	
Party	Party_Desc	FIN001	Customer	Customer_Public_Name	Hardcode	
Party	Party_Date_Of_Birth	FIN001	CONSTANT	NULL	Hardcode	
Party	Party_Start_Dttm	FIN001	CONSTANT	Customer_Start_Dt	Transformation	If a row already exists in Target table then update the Target row only if date provided in source is less than Target date, else ignore
Party	Party_Subtype	FIN001	CONSTANT	"2"	Hardcode	"2 for "ORGANIZATION"
Party	Party_Department	FIN001	CONSTANT	NULL	Hardcode	

*TRN CAT, Transformation Category.

Source
Consider the following two tables in staging:

1. CONSUMER_BILL containing information about a consumer's bill
2. CONSUMER_BILL_DUE_DATE containing information about the date when the consumer's bill is due

Target
The target of this source data is the INVOICE table containing columns shown in Figure 12.2.

Mapping
First and foremost, mapping is done to ensure that both source tables contain the required information. If not, then a special rule needs to be applied to handle this issue (Table 12.2).

Now consider that the source data is not synchronized. For such a scenario, there are multiple options:

1. Use the left outer join, keeping CONSUMER_BILL on the left side and lose CONSUMER_BILL_DUE_DATE information.
2. Use the full outer join and, when merging data into target table, populate only NOT NULL target columns.

In real life, data in source tables is mostly unsynchronized, and the data mapper must create rules to handle this. We need to ensure that we try to load all source information in target tables.

INVOICE

Invoice_Id
Invoice_Date
Invoice_Amount
Invoice_Billing_Id
Invoice_Due_Date
Invoice_Late_Charges

Figure 12.2 Target table for the data joining scenario.

Table 12.2 Data Mapping for the Data Joining Scenario

Target Table	Target Column	Record Id	Source Table	Source Column	TRN CAT*	Transformation Rule
INVOICE		CON001	CONSUMER_BILL CONSUMER_BILL_DUE_DATE		+	Join both tables using inner join on Bill_Id
INVOICE	Invoice Id	CON001	CONSUMER_BILL	Bill_Id	Direct	
INVOICE	Invoice Date	CON001	CONSUMER_BILL	Bill_Time	Direct	
INVOICE	Invoice Amount	CON001	CONSUMER_BILL	amt	Direct	
INVOICE	Invoice Billing Id	CON001	CONSTANT	NULL	Hardcode	
INVOICE	Invoice Due Date	CON001	CONSUMER_BILL_DUE_DATE		Direct	
INVOICE	Invoice Late charges	CON001	CONSUMER_BILL_DUE_DATE		Direct	

*TRN CAT, Transformation Category.

Last, there could be a possibility of having multiple rows in source tables. Reasons could be:

1. Multiple extracts are loaded in single execution.
2. Data quality issue
3. Source table structure

In such a case, add a rule to take only one row from the source table. The simplest way is to use qualifying statements. In the header rule, add the following text: "In case there are multiple rows for one Bill_Id in source tables, select the latest row based on extraction date."

DATA INTEGRATION FROM MULTIPLE SOURCES (NORMALIZED MODEL)

In almost all organizations, the same data is available from multiple sources. This provides better data quality and coverage for a data warehouse. However, at the same time, it creates complexity in the ETL process and data mapping.

We need a process that gives high priority to a source over the other. Think about having more than two sources and prioritizing data per table.

No matter how difficult and complex it is, the end result is information that is complete and of the best possible quality, giving the client the power to use it for reporting benefits.

In this mapping, we will discuss a prioritization process that can be used for all mappings in the target table.

Source

In this scenario, we will map data for televisions that are manufactured by the client and store the data in the ITEM INSTANCE table. Consider the following sources and tables:

1. The first source is the manufacturing system used in factories; the table name is Manufac_Detail.
2. The second source is a testing system, where data is inserted after testing is carried out; the table name is Device_QA.
3. The third source is a sales system, where data is populated after a television is sold to a customer; the table name is Sale.

ITEM_INSTANCE

Item_Instance_Id
Item_Instance_Date Item_Type_Cd Item_Instance_Color Item_Instance_Size Item_Instance_Technology Item_Instance_Location Item_Instance_Category_Cd

Figure 12.3 Target table for the data integration scenario.

Because of the different nature of all three systems, we will have multiple columns in each table. We will be using them based on target table requirements.

Target
The target in this scenario is the ITEM INSTANCE table, where information regarding instances of an item will be stored. In this case, television manufacturing data will be loaded in this table. This table is slightly denormalized to show how different sources provide the same information (Figure 12.3).

Mapping
Table 12.3 shows the mapping for all three sources to ITEM INSTANCE. In this example, we only needed source table-level priority, so we defined it at the header level. As it can be seen in the table, one source has been defined as the master for ITEM INSTANCE and the other two as negative or secondary sources. The priority is defined in the header, which is later used to merge load-ready data into the EDW table.

DATA QUALITY IMPROVEMENT
Although the quality of the data cannot be controlled by the data warehouse, there are many cases when well-defined rules can be used to improve data quality. The ideal situation is that the data warehouse team reports data quality issues to the source, and the source fixes the issue. In some cases, this is either not possible or there isn't enough

Table 12.3 Data Mapping for the Data Integration Scenario

Target Table	Target Column	Record Id	Source Table	Source Column	TRN CAT*	Transformation Rule
ITEM INSTANCE		MAN001	MANUF_DETAIL		+	P = 100
ITEM INSTANCE	Item Instance Id	MAN001	MANUF_DETAIL	TV_Production_No	Direct	
ITEM INSTANCE	Item Instance Date	MAN001	MANUF_DETAIL	Manuf_Time	Direct	
ITEM INSTANCE	Item Instance Color	MAN001	MANUF_DETAIL	Production_Color	Direct	
ITEM INSTANCE	Item Instance Size	MAN001	MANUF_DETAIL	Screen_Size	Hardcode	
ITEM INSTANCE	Item Instance Technology	MAN001	MANUF_DETAIL	TV_Type	Direct	
ITEM INSTANCE	Item Instance Location	MAN001	MANUF_DETAIL	Factory Production_Line	Transformation	
ITEM INSTANCE	Item Instance Category Cd	MAN001	CONSTANT	"1"	Hardcode	– "1" for television
ITEM INSTANCE		MAN001	DEVICE_QA		–	P = 80
ITEM INSTANCE	Item Instance Id	MAN001	DEVICE_QA	TV_Id	Direct	
ITEM INSTANCE	Item Instance Date	MAN001	DEVICE_QA	TV_Created	Direct	
ITEM INSTANCE	Item Instance Color	MAN001	CONSTANT	NULL	Hardcode	
ITEM INSTANCE	Item Instance Size	MAN001	CONSTANT	NULL	Hardcode	
ITEM INSTANCE	Item Instance Technology	MAN001	CONSTANT	NULL	Hardcode	
ITEM INSTANCE	Item Instance Location	MAN001	CONSTANT	NULL	Hardcode	
ITEM INSTANCE	Item Instance Category Cd	MAN001	CONSTANT	"1"	Hardcode	– "1" for television
ITEM INSTANCE		MAN001	SALE		–	P = 90 WHERE Sold_Item_Type = "Television"
ITEM INSTANCE	Item Instance Id	MAN001	SALE	Sold_Item_Id	Direct	
ITEM INSTANCE	Item Instance Date	MAN001	SALE	Sold_Time	Direct	
ITEM INSTANCE	Item Instance Color	MAN001	SALE	Sold_Item_Color	Direct	
ITEM INSTANCE	Item Instance Size	MAN001	SALE	Sold_Item_Size	Direct	
ITEM INSTANCE	Item Instance Technology	MAN001	SALE	Item_Sub_Class	Direct	
ITEM INSTANCE	Item Instance Location	MAN001	CONSTANT	NULL	Hardcode	
ITEM INSTANCE	Item Instance Category Cd	MAN001	CONSTANT	"1"	Hardcode	– "1" for Television

time. In such cases, the analyst or client SME will suggest rules for data quality improvement.

Source

Let's take an example of a cell phone manufacturing client. The client has a unique identification system called DSN (Device Serial Number) for its devices and gives every device manufactured a unique ID. There is also an international standard for identifying every cell phone uniquely. This code is called IMEI (International Mobile station Equipment Identity).

In this scenario, we have two sources. The first one gives the relationship between DSN and IMEI. The second source gives data about warranty claims for both DSN and IMEI. But most of the time, DSN is either null or contains garbage data.

In EDW, DSN is used to uniquely identify an instance of cell phone; hence, it is not acceptable to have NULLs or garbage data in this column. Ideally, the source should provide us this information, but let's assume that this cannot be done.

A warranty claim row is generated when a consumer comes to a shop and submits the device for repair. But because these shops or repair centers can be anywhere around the globe, ensuring DSN value availability is difficult. On the other hand, all employees know about an IMEI, and this information is correctly populated in the source.

Target

ITEM INSTANCE IDENTIFICATION will be used to store the relationship between a DSN and IMEI (Figure 12.4).

Mapping

See Table 12.4.

Here, we are trying to get best possible value from the source. Ideally, we should get a row from ITEM INST IDENTIFICATION as a device is manufactured and then repaired if required. Even if repair doesn't happen, the DSN values should be in compliance with the client's established rules (the first three characters are letters, and the total length is more than eight), and only "valid value" should be inserted. If this is not the case, then insert "UNKNOWN."

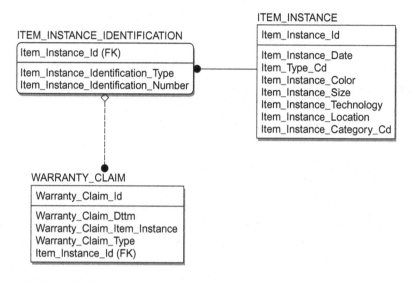

Figure 12.4 Target table for the data quality improvement scenario.

PRIORITIZED DATA CONSOLIDATION OR JOINING

Most of the time, data mapping includes simple joins between tables to create the target dataset. But there are cases when a complex priority system is required to join two tables of the source. These kinds of cases can emerge when the client's data is not connected through a well-defined identification process and the data mapper needs to create transformation rules to join two datasets.

Source data in such cases can be of bad quality, and the expected outcome of the join is a low rate of success. Yet the business case requires this transformation, and the data mapper has to get the maximum out of this mapping.

Source
Let's take example of a publisher that maintains different data sources and wants to combine data to get a single picture of the organization. Two of the client's datasets are:

1. **Mailing list:** The client maintains a mailing list on which it sends news and updates. Consumers can join different mailing lists by filling in a form online or through other means. Data quality can be bad in this case because consumers might input wrong information and give only the correct email address. This is a common scenario

Table 12.4 Data Mapping for the Data Quality Improvement Scenario

Target Table	Target Column	Record Id	Source Table	Source Column	TRN CAT*	Transformation Rule
ITEM INSTANCE IDENTIFICATION		MAN001	MANUF_DETAIL		+	P = 100
ITEM INSTANCE IDENTIFICATION	Item Instance Id	MAN001	MANUF_DETAIL	DSN	Direct	
ITEM INSTANCE IDENTIFICATION	Item Instance Identification Type	MAN001	MANUF_DETAIL	IMEI	Direct	
ITEM INSTANCE IDENTIFICATION	Item Instance Identification Number	MAN001	CONSTANT	"1"	Direct	– "1" is for IMEI
ITEM INSTANCE		CLA001	Claim		–	P = 30 Join with ITEM INST IDENTIFICATION on SOURCE.IMEI = Item Instance Identification Number and Item Instance Identification Type = 1 If a row is found then ignore this row. Else insert a row only if DSN column length is greater than 8 and first three characters are alphabet letters. Use uppercase and trim.
ITEM INSTANCE	Item Instance Id	CLA001	Claim	DSN IMEI	Transformation	UPPER(TRIM(DSN)) See header rule for filtering of data

(Continued)

Table 12.4 (Continued)

Target Table	Target Column	Record Id	Source Table	Source Column	TRN CAT*	Transformation Rule
ITEM INSTANCE	Item Instance Date	CLA001	Claim	Claim_Dt	Direct	
WARRANTY CLAIM		CLA001	Claim		+	P = 100 CLAIM a Left join ITEM INSTANCE IDENTIFICATION b ON a. IMEI = b. Item Instance Identification Number AND b. Item Instance Identification = 1
WARRANTY CLAIM	Warranty Claim Id	CLA001	Claim	Claim_Id	Direct	
WARRANTY CLAIM	Warranty Claim Dttm	CLA001	Claim	Claim_Dt	Direct	
WARRANTY CLAIM	Warranty Claim Item Instance	CLA001	Claim	IMEI DSN	Transformation	CASE WHEN B.Item Instance Id IS NOT NULL THEN B.Item Instance Id WHEN length (A. DSN) >8 AND substr(A. DSN,1,3) is alphanumeric THEN UPPER(TRIM(DSN)) ELSE "UNKNOWN" END
WARRANTY CLAIM	Warranty Claim Type	CLA001	CONSTANT	"1"	Hardcode	

TRN CAT. Transformation Category.

as organizations want to grow their reach to clients and allow consumers to get in touch without formal accounts.

2. **Order delivery system:** The second source system stores data about order fulfillment. Consumers order products, and the client delivers them. In this case, the client maintains complete information about the client, and data quality is good because the payment is done based on the client's real name, and the product will be delivered only to the correct address.

Although the second source system has an identification system of the individual, it cannot be joined with the first source because there is no identification column available there. From the client's perspective, they want to know how many consumers ordered a product after receiving a communication (mailing list).

Target
In this scenario, our target table is a surrogate key table where we flag a consumer with source system if we find matching data (Figure 12.5).

Mapping
A data mapper's focus in this scenario should be to that the ensure maximum possible data is joined and identified. Not having a column

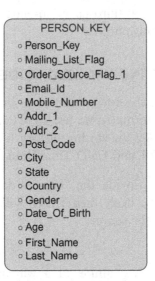

Figure 12.5 Target table for the priority-based data scenario.

to join makes it difficult to correlate data, but we will use a priority-based approach for matching data.

The first and most accurate way to link users from both systems is to see whether the email address is the same. Below is one way of defining the priority.

1. Email address
2. Normalized telephone or cell phone number
3. Normalized address and name
4. Complete name and date of birth
5. Complete name and age
6. Complete name and gender
7. Complete name (Table 12.5)

Normalization is mandatory in this scenario as it will increase the chances of matching data. For example, in the case of a cell phone number, some data might contain country codes, spaces, parentheses, or zeros at the start. Before joining data, the data mapper should make sure that values from both systems are normalized and can be joined.

Addresses can also be standardized based on well-defined rules. In some countries, addresses are well defined and are based on a standard patterns, but still some users fill in values that cannot be joined directly. In such cases, either the data mapper can define rules for normalizing values, or a third-party application program interface (API) can be used for this purpose.

HISTORY HANDLING (NORMALIZED MODEL)

Data warehouses not only store transactions but also track changes in an entity's attributes. Normally, we use Type 2 slowly changing dimension (SCD) methodology for storing history (i.e., keeping all changes in the table with START and END Time/Date columns).

The source should provide the time or date when change takes place. If this is not the case, then EDW will use the time when it received the data from the source.

Source

In this case, consider an example of a warranty claim, in which a device is repaired multiple times before it is fixed, discarded, or

Table 12.5 Data Mapping for the Priority-Based Data Scenario

Target Table	Target Column	Source Table	Source Column	TRN CAT*	Transformation Rule
PERSON_KEY		MailList			Update old row by setting Mailing_List_Flag = 1 if there is a match based on below priority. Else insert a new row. 1. Email address 2. Normalized telephone/mobile number 3. Normalized address and name 4. Complete name and date of birth 5. Complete name and age 6. Complete name and gender 7. Complete name
PERSON_KEY	Person_Key	EDW		Transformation	
PERSON_KEY	Mailing_List_Flag	MailList		Transformation	
PERSON_KEY	Order_Source_Flag	MailList		Transformation	
PERSON_KEY	Email_id	MailList	Email_id	Transformation	
PERSON_KEY	Mobile_Number	MailList	Mobile_Number	Transformation	Normalize mobile_number values to standard phone number i.e., 00XYYYYZZZZZZZ where X is country number, YYYY is area/operator identifier, and ZZZZZZZZ is actual number of user
PERSON_KEY	Addr_1	MailList	Address	Transformation	Normalize address from source to standard address format
PERSON_KEY	Addr_2	MailList	Address	Transformation	Normalize address from source to standard address format
PERSON_KEY	Post_Code	MailList	Post_Code	Transformation	
PERSON_KEY	City	MailList	City	Transformation	
PERSON_KEY	State	MailList	State	Transformation	Normalize data to short form of state code.

(Continued)

Table 12.5 (Continued)

Target Table	Target Column	Source Table	Source Column	TRN CAT*	Transformation Rule
PERSON_KEY	Country	MailList	Country	Direct	
PERSON_KEY	Gender	MailList	Gender	Transformation	Convert source data into single letter form using below codes M Male F Female U Unknown
PERSON_KEY	Date_Of_Birth	MailList	Date_Of_Birth	Transformation	Convert to Date
PERSON_KEY	Age	MailList	Age	Transformation	If source column is null then calculate age based on date_of_birth
PERSON_KEY	First_Name	MailList	Name	Transformation	Convert full name to first name and last name
PERSON_KEY	Last_Name	MailList	Name	Transformation	Convert full name to first name and last name
PERSON_KEY		OrderFulSys			Update old row by setting Order_Source_Flag = 1 if there is a match based on below priority. Else insert a new row. 1. Email address 2. Normalized telephone/mobile number 3. Normalized address and name 4. Complete name and date of birth 5. Complete name and age 6. Complete name and gender 7. Complete name
PERSON_KEY	Person_Key	EDW		Transformation	
PERSON_KEY	Mailing_List_Flag	OrderFulSys		Transformation	
PERSON_KEY	Order_Source_Flag	OrderFulSys		Transformation	
PERSON_KEY	Email_id	OrderFulSys	Email_id	Transformation	

PERSON_KEY	Mobile_Number	OrderFulSys	Mobile_Number	Transformation	Normalize mobile_number values to standard phone number i.e., 00XYYYYZZZZZZZZ where X is country number, YYYY is area/operator identifier, and ZZZZZZZZ is actual number of user
PERSON_KEY	Addr_1	OrderFulSys	Address	Transformation	Normalize address from source to standard address format
PERSON_KEY	Addr_2	OrderFulSys	Address	Transformation	Normalize address from source to standard address format
PERSON_KEY	Post_Code	OrderFulSys	Post_Code	Transformation	
PERSON_KEY	City	OrderFulSys	City	Transformation	
PERSON_KEY	State	OrderFulSys	State	Transformation	Normalize data to short form of state code
PERSON_KEY	Country	OrderFulSys	Country	Direct	
PERSON_KEY	Gender	MailList	Gender	Transformation	Convert source data into single letter form using below codes M Male F Female U Unknown
PERSON_KEY	Date_Of_Birth	MailList	Date_Of_Birth	Transformation	Convert to Date
PERSON_KEY	Age	MailList	Age	Transformation	If source column is null then calculate age based on date_of_birth
PERSON_KEY	First_Name	OrderFulSys	FirstName	Direct	
PERSON_KEY	Last_Name	OrderFulSys	LastName	Direct	

*TRN CAT, Transformation Category.

EVENT_STATUS

Event_Id
Event_Status_Type_Cd
Event_Status_Start_Dttm
Event_Status_End_Dttm
Event_Status_Cd

Figure 12.6 Target table for the normalized history-handling scenario.

repaired again. The source will provide this information. It might provide multiple statuses in one extract or in multiple extracts. EDW should handle all possible scenarios.

Target
The target of this table is EVENT STATUS. We will track the status of the device repair at the claim level (Figure 12.6).

Mapping
For history-handled mappings, it is mandatory to mark the columns for which change is captured. The primary key of the table would contain additional columns that might not be part of the columns for which change in nonprimary key columns is captured (Table 12.6).

History-handling rules need to explain all possible scenarios. They should take care of:

1. Loading anomalies (e.g., backdated data sent by the source)
2. Missing date or time information
3. Special cases specific to the source or table

HISTORY HANDLING DONE IN THE SOURCE (NORMALIZED MODEL)

There can be cases when the source is providing history-handled data and the EDW needs to make sure that the source's history is maintained in the EDW. This can be simpler than history handling done inside EDW but needs careful interpretation of the source data to make sure that there is no gap or overlap.

Table 12.6 Data Mapping for the Normalized History-Handling Scenario

Target Table	Target Column	Record Id	Source Table	Source Column	TRN CAT*	Transformation Rule
EVENT STATUS		CLA001	Claim_Status	Claim_Status	+	P = 100
EVENT STATUS	Event Id	CLA001	Claim_Status	Claim_Id	Direct	
EVENT STATUS	Status Type Cd	CLA001	CONSTANT	"1"	Hardcode	– "1" for status of Claims
EVENT STATUS	Status Start Dttm	CLA001	Claim_Status	ClaimUpdatedTime	Transformation	Use Current System Time if NULL
EVENT STATUS	Event Status End Dttm	CLA001	History Handling		Transformation	Track History for Event Id and Event Status Type Cd when Event Status Cd changes Rules to be observed: 1. If current EDW status equals received new extract then ignore new row. 2. If multiple statuses are received in same extract then insert all in EDW table without duplicate of status sequence. 3. If old statuses are received (due to back dated data) then insert old row making sure that there is no gap or overlap due to this row. 4. When Claim_Status value lies in "Pass", "Discarded" then close event with no repair attempts. Close last record, setting Event Status End Dttm = Claim_Updated_Time
EVENT STATUS	Event Status Cd	CLA001	Claim_Status	Claim_Status	Direct	

TRN CAT, Transformation Category.

EVENT_STATUS

Event_Id
Event_Status_Type_Cd
Event_Status_Start_Dttm
Event_Status_End_Dttm
Event_Status_Cd

Figure 12.7 Target table for the source history-handling scenario.

Source
Let's take the same example of a warranty claim. This time history handling of change in status column is done by the source.

Target
See Figure 12.7.

Mapping
See Table 12.7.

HISTORY HANDLING WITH NO RULES ON DATE OR TIME
Some history-handling requirements in data warehousing cannot be treated in terms of SCD types and require special rules.

Source
The best example of this type of case is from the telecom sector, where a subscriber can get bundles or bonus resources for a certain time.

1. The bundle can expire after the time limit is reached.
2. The resource limit can be reached (e.g., 100 free minutes are used before expiry).
3. The same product is subscribed to again before expiry.
4. The user subscribes to a product that has an expiry of 1 year, but he leaves the operator.

EDW needs to make sure that all of these cases are treated accordingly and that the correct start and end time are set. Because this is not traditional history handling, the product start and end times are still tracked.

Table 12.7 Data Mapping for the Source History-Handling Scenario

Target Table	Target Column	Record Id	Source Table	Source Column	TRN CAT*	Transformation Rule
EVENT STATUS		CLA001	Claim_Status		+	P = 100
						Source provides status history to confirm source inserts/ updates are stored. Updates in source can bring complexity in EDW. However, since source is tracking history, EDW needs to make sure any changes in time window source are reflected in EDW.
						To achieve this, EDW will identify whether a row received from source overlaps with historical data stored in EDW. If there is overlap EDW will delete the rows and insert new source rows. In this table, defining a primary key of source data is not possible because of changing start/end time. EDW will have only one option, i.e., identify overlaps and try to identify the change in source.
						Overlap in time window is only way a change in source is identified. Once change is identified, EDW removes old rows lying in this overlap and inserts change from the source. Since history handling is done insource, it does not create gaps/ overlaps.
EVENT STATUS	Event Id	CLA001	Claim_Status	Claim_Id	Direct	
EVENT STATUS	Event Status Type Cd	CLA001	CONSTANT	"1"	Hardcode	– "1" for status of Claims
EVENT STATUS	Event Status Start Dttm	CLA001	Claim_Status	Status_Created_Tm	Direct	
EVENT STATUS	Event Status End Dttm	CLA001	History Handling	Status_Closed_Tm	Direct	
EVENT STATUS	Event Status Cd	CLA001	Claim_Status	Claim_Status	Direct	

TRN CAT, Transformation Category.

PRODUCT_SUBSCRIPTION

Subscription_Start_Dttm
User_Mobile_Number
Product_Id
Subscription_Ens_Dttm
Subscription_Status_Cd

Figure 12.8 Target table for the no-rule-date history-handling scenario.

Target

For simplicity, we will store the cell phone number in the User Mobile Number columns and the subscribed product, bundle, or offer in the Product Id columns (Figure 12.8).

Mapping

The mapping shown in Table 12.8 explains in detail what to do in different cases.

JOINING THE SOURCE DATA WITH THE TARGET TABLE

When making a decision about joins in the source system, it is sometimes not possible to join transactional data of the source with the master data of the source; there could be many reasons for this problem, including:

1. **Data quality:** Data quality is major problem in data warehouse success, as discussed throughout this book. If the source data is of bad quality, then we apply special transformation rules to improve the quality of the data in the target table. For master data, we usually rely on good sources to load target tables and ignore dirty sources, or we apply rules to fix dirty data. When we compare the source versus the target for our join in transformation, we have to use the target table to ensure that our joins meet business requirements.
2. **Business logic:** If the source system doesn't provide complete data and the only way to complete transformation of the source data is to use the target table, then we use a join with the target tables. For example, the source provides employees' information but doesn't provide employees' current status. The status of the employees is stored in a target loaded from another source system. In this case, we will join the source with the target to get the final transformed data.
3. **Data completeness:** If the source data contains partial data and transformation (aggregations or lookup) requires a complete

Table 12.8 Data Mapping for the No-Rule-Date History Handling Scenario

Target Table	Target Column	Record Id	Source Table	Source Column	TRN CAT*	Transformation Rule
PRODUCT SUBSCRIPTION		MED001	Product_Operation		+	Use below History Handling Rule after Transformation (in Apply phase) Case 1: Un-Subscription Select all rows where Subscription Status Cd = 1. This will give you un-subscriptions. Find this subscription in Target table for combination of (User Mobile Number and Product Id) and set Subscription End Dttm = Tmstmp Case 2: Expiry Select all rows where Subscription Status Cd = 2. This will give expiries. Find this subscription in target table for combination of (User Mobile Number and Product Id) and set Subscription End Dttm = Tmstmp Case 3: Subscription and Re-Subscription Select all rows where Subscription Status Cd = 0. This will give subscriptions of new products. Check if there exists a row in EDW that has END DTTM less than START DTTM of source. This will give subscriptions that happened before expiry of previous subscriptions. Close previous record and insert new one. In case no row is found then insert the new one only There are chances that subscription/insubscriptions/expiry/multiple subscriptions happen in a single extract. The code should close-open records accordingly

(Continued)

Table 12.8 (Continued)

Target Table	Target Column	Record Id	Source Table	Source Column	TRN CAT*	Transformation Rule
PRODUCT SUBSCRIPTION	User Mobile Number	MED001	Product_Operation	MSISDN	Direct	
PRODUCT SUBSCRIPTION	Product Id	MED001	Product_Operation	Prod_Nm	Direct	
PRODUCT SUBSCRIPTION	Subscription Start Dttm	MED001	Product_Operation	Tmstamp	Direct	
PRODUCT SUBSCRIPTION	Subscription End Dttm	MED001	History Handling		Direct	
PRODUCT SUBSCRIPTION	Subscription Status Cd	MED001	Product_Operation	Operation Id	Direct	– Lookup values 0 Subscription 1 Un-subscription 2 Expiry
PRODUCT SUBSCRIPTION		MED001	MSISDN_DUMP		+	Select rows where MSISDN_STATUS = "SUSPENDED" Use the MSISDN and close all open records
PRODUCT SUBSCRIPTION	User Mobile Number	MED001	MSISDN_DUMP	MSISDN	Direct	
PRODUCT SUBSCRIPTION	Product Id	MED001			Direct	
PRODUCT SUBSCRIPTION	Subscription Start Dttm	MED001			Direct	
PRODUCT SUBSCRIPTION	Subscription End Dttm	MED001	Direct	MSISDN_Status_Time	Direct	
PRODUCT SUBSCRIPTION	Subscription Status Cd	MED001	CONSTANT	"3"	Direct	– "3" Product expired Subscriber Leaving

*TRN CAT, Transformation Category.

Table 12.9 Source Data for the Target Join Scenario		
Employee Id	Name	Address
1	John	London
2	Peter	Paris
3	Alecia	Karachi

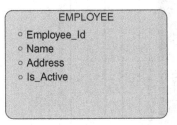

EMPLOYEE
○ Employee_Id
○ Name
○ Address
○ Is_Active

Figure 12.9 Data mapping for the target join scenario.

dataset, then we join with the target table to get access to the complete data set. An example may be master data from the source. If the source contains only active users and the join requires all users, then we will join with the target table to get access to all users.

Source
For this scenario we will discuss a business logic case for understanding the concept. The source in this case contains employees' data (Table 12.9).

Target
The target in this case requires employees' personal data along with their most recent employment status (Figure 12.9).

Mapping
Because the source doesn't provide the employees' status, we will use a target table to populate this column. The target table used in this case is EMPLOYEE_STATUS loaded from another source (Table 12.10).

Joins with the target table are inevitable and are required in enterprise-level data warehouse implementations to fulfill business requirements.

Table 12.10 Data Mapping for Target Join Scenario

Target Table	Target Column	Source System	Source Table	Source Column	Transformation Rule
EMPLOYEE		ADMIN_DBO	EMP		
EMPLOYEE	Employee_Id	ADMIN_DBO	EMP	Employee_Id	
EMPLOYEE	Name	ADMIN_DBO	EMP	Name	
EMPLOYEE	Address	ADMIN_DBO	EMP	Address	
EMPLOYEE	Status	EDW	EMPLOYEE_STATUS	Status_Id	Look up this employee_Id in EMPLOYEE STATUS and get latest status by filtering on Employee_Status_End_Date = "9999-12-31 23:59:59"

Table 12.11 Source Data for the Snapshot History-Handling Scenario					
Employee Id	Snapshot Date	Name	Married	Address	Salary
1	1/1/2017	Alecia	N	London	10
1	1/2/2017	Alecia	N	London	10
1	1/3/2017	Alecia	N	London	10
1	1/4/2017	Alecia	N	Paris	10
1	1/5/2017	Alecia	N	Paris	10
1	1/6/2017	Alecia	N	Paris	10
1	1/7/2017	Alecia Carpenter	Y	Paris	10
1	1/8/2017	Alecia Carpenter	Y	Paris	10
1	1/9/2017	Alecia Carpenter	Y	Paris	10
1	1/10/2017	Alecia Carpenter	Y	Paris	20

HISTORY HANDLING FROM SNAPSHOTS

Some source systems maintain snapshots of their data on a predefined frequency. Snapshot frequency depends on the source's requirement and is not directly meant for data warehousing. Based on the business requirements of the data warehouse, we have to create time windows from these snapshots.

If the primary key of the snapshot and target table is the same, then the logic is simple—we identify when there was a change in the source data and take that row to the data warehouse, ignoring the rest of the data.

Source
Consider an administrative source system where employee information is stored and the system takes a snapshot of the data every day (Table 12.11).

Target
In this scenario, we will map source snapshots to three target tables. The main table, EMPLOYEE, will store master data, and the other two tables will maintain a history of the employees' attributes (Figure 12.10).

Mapping
The first thing we have to do is to think of the delta and initial loads separately. Daily or delta loading is simple because we need to

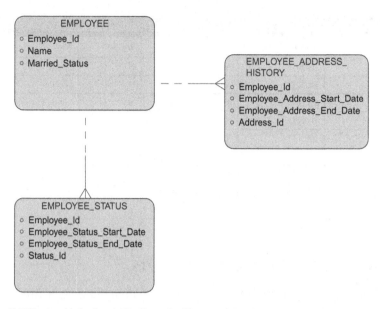

Figure 12.10 Target table for the snapshot history-handling scenario.

Table 12.12 Data Mapping for the Snapshot History-Handling Scenario					
Employee Id	**Snapshot Date**	**Name**	**Married**	**Address**	**Salary**
1	1/1/2017	Alecia	N	London	10
1	1/4/2017	Alecia	N	Paris	10

compare a snapshot row with the latest row in the target to see if there is any change in the source for transformation.

However, in the initial load, we need to identify rows where data changed and treat it appropriately. We can create a single mapping or code for both cases, but it will make things complex, so it is recommended to create two separate mappings.

Let's discuss change in address for of the employee. From the data sample earlier, we can see that this employee moved only once to a new address on 2017-01-04; this means that all other rows of this table will be ignored for this mapping (Table 12.12).

The below SQL code gives a simple logic that can be used to get only those rows that have a change in source.

```
SELECT a.Employee_Id, a.Address, a.snapshotdate
FROM
(
   SELECT  Employee_Id, Address, snapshotdate, row_number () over (
PARTITION BY Employee_Id ORDER BY snapshotdate) rankk
   FROM EMPLOYEE_SNAPSHOT
   WHERE Address IS NOT NULL AND Employee_Id IS NOT NULL
) a
LEFT JOIN
(
   SELECT  Employee_Id, Address, snapshotdate, row_number () over (
PARTITION BY Employee_Id ORDER BY snapshotdate) rankk
   FROM EMPLOYEE_SNAPSHOT
   WHERE Address IS NOT NULL  AND Employee_Id IS NOT NULL
) b
ON a.Employee_Id = b.Employee_Id
AND a.rankk = b.rankk + 1
AND a.Address ! = b.Address
WHERE b.Employee_Id IS NOT NULL OR a.rankk = 1
```

Because the snapshot is incremental, we need to decide whether to ignore old data that came after we loaded later data. For example, if we have loaded the 2017-January snapshot data in the data warehouse and now receive 2014 data from source, we need to decide whether we will discard old data or if we will rebuild history in the data warehouse. This should be discussed with the client and a decision made to meet business requirements.

MASTER DATA (NORMALIZED MODEL)

Master data or reference data is as important as transactional or fact data. It is needed in reporting and provides dimensional insights for facts. Master data should come from a single source; it should be complete, clean, and historically accurate.

In some projects, the data steward creates this data for the data warehouse in a static source or data warehouse tables. This static data is augmented whenever new values are added (e.g., new products launched by the company, the company starts business in new country). In this case, the data warehouse doesn't need complex rules, so this data is simply loaded in the EDW.

In most projects, the EDW has to rely on source system data for populating its reference or master data tables. This creates a lot of complexity because getting full understanding of the client's business is not only difficult but sometimes impossible. The data mapper has to make the best out of what information is available and create mappings or rules to provide the best data in the EDW.

The real challenge here is data coming from transactional systems that is not received from the main source (e.g., a telecom subscriber starts making calls, but the master data will come later, and call records start coming to EDW in real time). These source systems create major challenges for designers with questions such as:

1. What will happen to the data that is already loaded in the EDW without master data?
2. What should be done with data for which master data has been updated in the master source but not reflected in the transactional system?
3. How should time-based master data from nonmaster sources be handled?
4. How should history for data that is coming from both master and transactional source systems be built?

All of these questions and other factors should be addressed by the data mapper. The logic will vary from project to project. A comprehensive analysis of the client's business working is required before the master data can be mapped.

Below are some examples that will give basic idea regarding mappings of master data. In real-life scenarios, data mapping should only be done after the data mapper has complete understanding of the source data.

Source
Let's take an example of a car manufacturer that has master data of cars coming from Design source table and manufacturing data coming from the Manuf. source table. The Design table will provide information about the company's designs of cars and their grouping.

The Manuf. table will provide information of all cars manufactured based on design.

Target
See Figure 12.11.

Mapping
We will map both the source data to these tables and see which rules are used to handle different complex issues.

Let's first see mappings of the main ITEM table from both sources. This is relatively easier because we will be using the master source for UPSERT and the secondary source for INSERT only (Table 12.13).

For cases in which history handling is done on master data, it is recommended not to use secondary or transactional systems to load data. If the SME guarantees or the data mapper can conclude from analysis that the transactional system is or will provide the correct data, then we can load this data in history-treated tables. Next, the design decision for the data mapper is what to do when there is

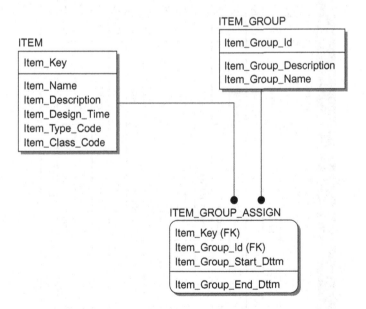

Figure 12.11 Target table for the master data scenario.

Table 12.13 Data Mapping for the Master Data Scenario 1

Target Table	Target Column	Record Id	Source Table	Source Column	TRN CAT*	Transformation Rule
ITEM		MAN001	MANUF		–	P = 80
ITEM	Item Key	MAN001	MANUF	Design_Cd	Direct	
ITEM	Item Name	MAN001	CONSTANT	NULL	Hardcode	
ITEM	Item Description	MAN001	CONSTANT	NULL	Hardcode	
ITEM	Item Design Time	MAN001	MANUF	Manuf_St	Direct	
ITEM	Item Type Code	MAN001	CONSTANT	"1"	Hardcode	– "1" Vehicle
ITEM	Item Class Code	MAN001	CONSTANT	"1"	Hardcode	– "3" Sedan Passenger
ITEM		DES001	DESIGN		+	P = 100
ITEM	Item Key	DES001	DESIGN	Design_Cd	Direct	
ITEM	Item Name	DES001	DESIGN	Design_Name	Direct	
ITEM	Item Description	DES001	DESIGN	Design_Desc	Direct	
ITEM	Item Design Time	DES001	DESIGN	Design_Comp_Tm	Hardcode	
ITEM	Item Type Code	DES001	CONSTANT	"1"	Hardcode	– "1" Vehicle
ITEM	Item Class Code	DES001	DESIGN	Design_Type	Direct	

*TRN CAT: Transformation Category.

overlap between two systems and they each give different values. In such a case, priority has to be given to the source that is more trustworthy.

For example, in our case study, assume that the design was made in 2012 JAN and therefore that design XYZ will be categorized as an SUV (sports utility vehicle). However, after manufacturing started, government rules changed in January 2013, and now the design XYZ is categorized as a mini-van. The design source system reflected the change in February 2013, and the manufacturing system started sending the new value in January 2013. Here, we have an overlap, and both sources are giving different values. Because we know what happened, it is easy to conclude that the manufacturing system is giving the correct value. As you might have noticed, the data mapper has to ask a lot of questions of the SME and needs to have comprehensive understanding of the client's business to make decisions. From first thought, the data mapper can declare the DESIGN source system as more authentic, but in reality, it was not the case (Table 12.14).

Table 12.14 Data Mapping for the Master Data Scenario 2				
Record Id	Source Table	Source Column	TRN CAT*	Transformation Rule
DES001	DESIGN		+	Do History Handling when Item Group Id change for Item Key
DES001	DESIGN	Design_Cd	Direct	
DES001	DESIGN	US_DMV_Group	Direct	
DES001	DESIGN	Design_Start_Dt	Direct	
DES001	DESIGN			
MAN001	MANUF		−	History Handling when Item Group Id changes for Item Key. If there is overlap records between DESIGN and MANUF source system data then Manufacturing data gets high priority and time windows have no overlaps.
MAN001	MANUF	Design_Cd	Direct	
MAN001	MANUF	DMV_Val	Direct	
MAN001	MANUF	Manuf_St	Direct	
MAN001	MANUF			
*TRN CAT, Transformation Category.				

These kinds of issues can also be seen in the telecom industry, where a subscriber buys a SIM card and starts making calls, but his master data might come later in that day to EDW.

In some cases, master sources might keep only the latest state of a logical entity, but history comes from a transactional source. A very good example of this case is different cell phones used by a subscriber to makes calls with the same SIM card. In the call record source system, you will receive the IMEI of every cell phone with calls, and from the master source, you will receive only the latest IMEI. Hence, it makes more sense to store historical data of a subscriber's device or cell phone from the call record system rather than the master source. Master data should be loaded from both types of sources to have a complete picture in EDW.

SURROGATE KEYS

A surrogate key is a unique key for an entity in the client's business or for an object in the database. Sometimes natural keys cannot be used to create a unique primary key of the table. This is when the data modeler or architect decides to use surrogate or helping keys for a table in the LDM.

Some benefits of surrogate keys are:

1. Surrogate keys do not change while the row exists.
2. Natural keys might change in the source (e.g., migration to a new system), making them useless in the data warehouse.
3. Surrogate keys have numeric data types, which provide excellent performance during data processing and business queries.
4. Code can be automated if surrogate keys are shared across tables, making the ETL process simpler.

Source

Let us consider a telecom client that receives call records data from a Mobile Switching Centre (MSC) and Intelligent Network (IN) source systems. A call may be uniquely identified using multiple columns such as calling number, called number, time of call, and type of call (depending on the client's business requirements). Based on the identified columns, we would generate surrogate tables mapping for MSC and IN source systems.

SURROGATE_CALL_RECORD

Call_Record_Id
Calling_Number Called_Number Call_Date Call_Time Call_Type Call_Source_Type

Figure 12.12 Target table for the surrogate key scenario.

Target

Our target in this case is a surrogate table that will hold source values and assign an incremental value to each record. Note that we have a column Call_Source_Type, which will help in differentiating between the same records coming from different systems. Ideally, a data warehouse should identify the same records coming from two systems; however, in reality, the same kind of call coming from two different systems cannot be correlated because of their time difference. As a result, most telecom clients would like to keep data separately, which will be matched at an aggregated level of reporting (Figure 12.12).

Mapping
See Table 12.15.

> Convert to Date rules: Most of the time, developers will complain about errors related to mismatch of data types. Make sure that you add data types of source and target columns and provide rules to convert if they are not implicitly converted.

Development of these mappings is fairly straightforward with a simple check to find out if a row exists in the target or not. If yes, then do nothing; if no, insert a new row.

CALL DETAIL RECORD (CDR) MAPPING

Telecom clients exchange high volumes of call data. Business enterprises get valuable insights from the call data, thus helping them to manipulate this priceless data to devise their business and marketing

Table 12.15 Data Mapping for the Surrogate Key Scenario

Target Table	Target Column	Record Id	Source Table	Source Column	TRN CAT*	Transformation Rule
S_CALL_RECORD	Call_Record_Id	IN001	IN		+	Generate new Call_Record_Id based on other 6 columns
S_CALL_RECORD	Call_Record_Id	IN001	ETL		Trans	Generate ids if source row doesn't exist in target
S_CALL_RECORD	Calling_Number	IN001	IN	Anum	Direct	
S_CALL_RECORD	Called_Number	IN001	IN	Bnum	Direct	
S_CALL_RECORD	Call_Date	IN001	IN	tm_Stamp	Trans	Convert to Date
S_CALL_RECORD	Call_Time	IN001	IN	tm_Stamp	Trans	Convert to Time
S_CALL_RECORD	Call_Type	IN001	IN	Event_Type_Id	Direct	
S_CALL_RECORD	Call_Source_Type	IN001	CONSTANT	"1"	Hardcode	– "1" Rated PrePaid Calls
S_CALL_RECORD		MSC01	MSC_CALL		+	Generate new Call_Record_Id based on other 6 columns
S_CALL_RECORD	Call_Record_Id	MSC001	ETL		Trans	Generate ids if source row doesn't exist in target
S_CALL_RECORD	Calling_Number	MSC001	MSC_CALL	MSC_COL_3	Direct	
S_CALL_RECORD	Called_Number	MSC001	MSC_CALL	MSC_COL_13	Direct	
S_CALL_RECORD	Call_Date	MSC001	MSC_CALL	MSC_time	Trans	Convert to Date
S_CALL_RECORD	Call_Time	MSC001	MSC_CALL	MSC_time	Trans	Convert to Time
S_CALL_RECORD	Call_Type	MSC001	CONSTANT	"1"	Hardcode	– "1" voice Call
S_CALL_RECORD	Call_Source_Type	MSC001	CONSTANT	"2"	Hardcode	– "1" Unrated MSC Calls
S_CALL_RECORD		MSC002	MSC_SMS		+	Generate new Call_Record_Id based on 6 columns
S_CALL_RECORD	Call_Record_Id	MSC002	ETL		Trans	Generate ids if source row doesn't exist in target

S_CALL_RECORD	Calling_Number	MSC002	MSC_SMS	MSC_COL_3	Direct	
S_CALL_RECORD	Called_Number	MSC002	MSC_SMS	MSC_COL_13	Direct	
S_CALL_RECORD	Call_Date	MSC002	MSC_SMS	MSC_time	Trans	Convert to Date
S_CALL_RECORD	Call_Time	MSC002	MSC_SMS	MSC_time	Trans	Convert to Time
S_CALL_RECORD	Call_Type	MSC002	CONSTANT	"2"	Hardcode	– "2" SMS
S_CALL_RECORD	Call_Source_Type	MSC002	CONSTANT	"1"	Hardcode	– "1" Un-Rated MSC Calls
S_CALL_RECORD		MSC003	MSC_DATA		+	Generate new Call_Record_Id based on 6 columns
S_CALL_RECORD	Call_Record_Id	MSC003	ETL		Trans	Generate Ids if source row doesn't exist in target
S_CALL_RECORD	Calling_Number	MSC003	MSC_DATA	MSC_COL_3	Direct	
S_CALL_RECORD	Called_Number	MSC003	MSC_DATA	MSC_COL_13	Direct	
S_CALL_RECORD	Call_Date	MSC003	MSC_DATA	MSC_time	Trans	Convert to Date
S_CALL_RECORD	Call_Time	MSC003	MSC_DATA	MSC_time	Trans	Convert to Time
S_CALL_RECORD	Call_Type	MSC003	CONSTANT	"3"	Hardcode	– "3" Data Sessions
S_CALL_RECORD	Call_Source_Type	MSC003	CONSTANT	"1"	Hardcode	– "1" Un-Rated MSC Calls

*TRN CAT, Transformation Category.

strategies. Loading of telecom data into a data warehouse requires specific rules and handling procedures. We will explain how mapping handles and addresses these telecom issues with the help of an example.

Source

In this case, the source is mediated or rated Call Detail Record (CDR) data.

Target

In this case, the target is the CALL RECORD table. We understand that this table should also contain other information, but to keep things simple and easy to understand, we confine our mapping to fewer columns (Figure 12.13).

Mapping

Note that we are joining with surrogate tables to generate data warehouse keys (Table 12.16). We are also trying to provide price plan information if the source doesn't do so. Last, we are converting the duration of calls into pulses (i.e., providing units used in calls based on "charge time units"). For example, if the duration of a call is 91 seconds and charging is done per 30 seconds, then "charge time units" used will be 4. Similarly, for data session, we are converting data volume into units of 64 KB.

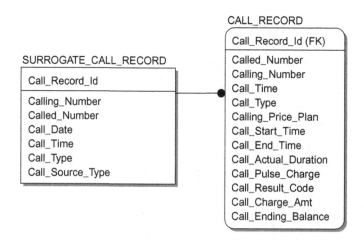

Figure 12.13 Target table for the telecom CDR data scenario.

Table 12.16 Data Mapping for the Telecom CDR Data Scenario

Target Table	Target Column	Record Id	Source Table	Source Column	TRN CAT*	Transformation Rule
CALL_RECORD		IN001	IN		+	Join source table as below IN IN LEFT JOIN S_CALL_RECORD SCR ON IN.Anum = SCR.Calling_Number AND IN.Bnum = SCR.Called_Number AND IN.tm_Stamp = SCR.Call_Date – convert source to Date AND IN.tm_Stamp = SCR.Call_Time – convert source to Time AND IN.Event_Type_Id = SCR.Call_Type AND SCR.Call_Source_Type = 1 LEFT JOIN Price_Plan PP ON PP.Price_Plan_Name = IN.pplan LEFT JOIN Subscriber_Price_Plan SPP ON SPP.Subscriber_Id = IN.Anum AND SPP.End_Dt IS NULL LEFT JOIN CALL_RESULT CR ON CR.Call_Result_Name = IN.Termination_Reason
CALL_RECORD	Call_Record_Id	IN001	S_CALL_RECORD		Trans	Generate Ids if source row doesn't exist in target
CALL_RECORD	Calling_Number	IN001	IN	Anum	Direct	
CALL_RECORD	Called_Number	IN001	IN	Bnum	Direct	
CALL_RECORD	Call_Start_Date	IN001	IN	Tm_Stamp	Trans	Convert to Date
CALL_RECORD	Call_Start_Time	IN001	IN	Tm_Stamp	Trans	Convert to Date
CALL_RECORD	Call_Type_Id	IN001	IN	Event_Type_Id	Direct	
CALL_RECORD	Call_End_Date	IN001	IN	Tm_Stamp Duration	Trans	Add Duration in Tm_Stamp and covert to Date
CALL_RECORD	Call_End_Time	IN001	IN	Tm_Stamp Duration	Trans	Add Duration in Tm_Stamp and covert to Time

(Continued)

Table 12.16 (Continued)

Target Table	Target Column	Record Id	Source Table	Source Column	TRN CAT*	Transformation Rule
CALL_RECORD	Calling_Price_Plan	IN001	Price_Plan pp Subscriber_Price_Plan Spp	Spp.Price_Plan_Id pp.Price_Plan_Id	Trans	Coalesce (pp.Price_Plan_Id,spp.Price_Plan_Id)
CALL_RECORD	Call_Actual_Duration	IN001	IN	Duration	Direct	
CALL_RECORD	Call_Pulse_Charge	IN001	IN	Duration	Trans	CASE Event_Type_Id WHEN 1 THEN CASE (pp.Price_Plan_Id,spp.Price_Plan_Id) WHEN 1 – 1 second billing THEN DURATION WHEN 2 – 30 second billing THEN Duration/30 + CASE WHEN Duration - (Cast (Duration/30 as Integer) * 30) > 0 THEN 1 ELSE 0 END ELSE DURATION/60 + CASE WHEN Duration - (Cast (Duration/60 as Integer) * 60) > 0 THEN 1 ELSE 0 END END WHEN 3 THEN VOLUME/64 + CASE WHEN VOLUME - (Cast (VOLUME /64 as Integer) * 64) > 0 THEN 1 ELSE 0 END – client charges @64kb ELSE COALESCE (DURATION,0) END
CALL_RECORD	Call_Charge_Amt	IN001	IN	Cost	Direct	
CALL_RECORD	Call_Ending_Balance	IN001	IN	Balance	Direct	
CALL_RECORD	Call_Result_Code	IN001	Call_Result CR	CR. Call_Result_Cd	LookUp	

*TRN CAT, Transformation Category.

PERFORMANCE ISSUE HANDLING IN MAPPING

Apart from logical mappings, the data mapper should also have a basic understanding of the database or ETL engine. This is required when optimizing code and changing mapping logic. Performance optimization is documented in data mapping whenever there is a change in transformation logic. If there is no room for performance improvement based on the current rules, then mapping should be updated and redesigned to address the performance issues.

We can divide single mapping into multiple mappings to divide the load or change the rules in the same mapping. From a data mapping perspective, any change made for performance optimization should be documented and should provide the same business results.

Source
Let's consider the same example that we have just discussed for the telecom client's call data. This is a very good example of high data volume during ETL loading that involves many joins with large tables.

Target
See Figure 12.14.

Mapping
In the following mapping, we have divided a single transformation into two. The idea is to divide joins into two sets to ensure that indexes

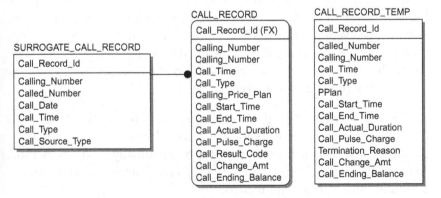

Figure 12.14 Target table for the performance issue scenario.

are used in the best possible way. We will not get into the details of performance tuning here, but here are some tips for a good start:

1. Try to separate the joins based on joining column; for example, one set could be the one having all joins based on calling number (Anum).
2. Try to divide bigger table joins into separate sets.
3. Identify a bigger table in which a nonindexed column is being used in a join. Extract the required data from this table into a temporary table and index the temporary table on the joining column.
4. Find a table that is causing product joins and check if you can reduce that table's data without using the product join. Sometime, a table might have multiple rows for the same joining column. This could be a data quality issue or could be caused by a primary key difference. If our logic allows, we can qualify this data into one row for one joining column value and store this resultset into a temporary table and later use that temporary table in a join with the source table.
5. Check if nulls are causing performance degradation, and if necessary, place conditions accordingly. For example, Coalesce (IN. columnname,'0') = tgt.columnname (Table 12.17)

BUSINESS MAPPING, REFERENCE, AND LOOKUP DATA (NORMALIZED MODEL)

Reference or lookup data is necessary for reporting because it provides business users with a method of identifying problems. For example, a business user can use the country code dimension to investigate further in case its revenue and sales are going down. In this way, countries that are not performing well may be identified, and based on this feedback, the business user may get back to the strategy to rectify the issues and improve performance.

The client should provide this reference data to avoid manual code handling within a data warehouse. In the absence of reference data, the data warehouse will either perform this manually or through code. As a result, both of these methods may create garbage, which might eventually show up in final reports.

Target Table	Target Column	Record Id	Source Table	Source Column	TRN CAT*	Transformation Rule
CALL_RECORD_TEMP		IN001	IN		+	Join source table as below IN IN LEFT JOIN S_CALL_RECORD SCR ON IN.Anum = SCR. Calling_Number AND IN.Bnum = SCR. Called_Number AND IN.tm_Stamp = SCR. Call_Date – convert source to Date AND IN.tm_Stamp = SCR. Call_Time – convert source to Time AND IN.Event_Type_Id = SCR. Call_Type AND SCR.Call_Source_Type = 1
CALL_RECORD_TEMP	Call_Record_Id	IN001	S_CALL_RECORD		Trans	Generate Ids if source row doesn't exist in target
CALL_RECORD_TEMP	Calling_Number	IN001	IN	Anum	Direct	
CALL_RECORD_TEMP	Called_Number	IN001	IN	Bnum	Direct	
CALL_RECORD_TEMP	Call_Start_Date	IN001	IN	tm_Stamp	Trans	Convert to Date
CALL_RECORD_TEMP	Call_Start_Time	IN001	IN	tm_Stamp	Trans	Convert to Date
CALL_RECORD_TEMP	Call_Type_Id	IN001	IN	Event_Type_Id	Direct	
CALL_RECORD_TEMP	Call_End_Date	IN001	IN	tm_Stamp Duration	Trans	Add Duration in Tm_Stamp and covert to Date
CALL_RECORD_TEMP	Call_End_Time	IN001	IN	tm_Stamp Duration	Trans	Add Duration in Tm_Stamp and covert to Time
CALL_RECORD_TEMP	Calling_Price_Plan	IN001	IN	pplan	Direct	
CALL_RECORD_TEMP	Call_Actual_Duration	IN001	IN	Duration	Direct	

(Continued)

Table 12.17 (Continued)

Target Table	Target Column	Record Id	Source Table	Source Column	TRN CAT*	Transformation Rule
CALL_RECORD_TEMP	Call_Pulse_Charge	IN001	IN	Duration	Trans	CASE Event_Type_Id WHEN 1 THEN CASE (pp.Price_Plan_Id,spp. Price_Plan_Id) WHEN 1 – 1 second billing THEN DURATION WHEN 2 – 30 second billing THEN Duration/30 + CASE WHEN Duration – (Cast (Duration/30 as Integer) * 30) > 0 THEN 1 ELSE 0 END ELSE DURATION/60 + CASE WHEN Duration - (Cast (Duration/60 as Integer) * 60) > 0 THEN 1 ELSE 0 END END WHEN 3 THEN DURATION/64 + CASE WHEN Duration - (Cast (Duration/64 as Integer) * 64) > 0 THEN 1 ELSE 0 END – client charges @64 kb ELSE COALESCE (DURATION,0) END
CALL_RECORD_TEMP	Call_Charge_Amt	IN001	IN	Cost	Direct	
CALL_RECORD_TEMP	Call_Ending_Balance	IN001	IN	Balance	Direct	
CALL_RECORD_TEMP	Call_Result_Code	IN001	IN	Termination_Reason	Direct	

CALL_RECORD	Call_Record_Id	IN001	CALL_RECORD_TEMP	Call_Record_Id	Direct	
CALL_RECORD	Calling_Number	IN001	CALL_RECORD_TEMP	Calling_Number	Direct	
CALL_RECORD	Called_Number	IN001	CALL_RECORD_TEMP	Called_Number	Direct	
CALL_RECORD	Call_Start_Date	IN001	CALL_RECORD_TEMP	Call_Start_Date	Direct	
CALL_RECORD	Call_Start_Time	IN001	CALL_RECORD_TEMP	Call_Start_Time	Direct	
CALL_RECORD	Call_Type_Id	IN001	CALL_RECORD_TEMP	Call_Type_Id	Direct	
CALL_RECORD	Call_End_Date	IN001	CALL_RECORD_TEMP	Call_End_Date	Direct	
CALL_RECORD	Call_End_Time	IN001	CALL_RECORD_TEMP	Call_End_Time	Direct	
CALL_RECORD	Calling_Price_Plan	IN001	Price_Plan pp Subscriber_Price_Plan Spp	spp.Price_Plan_Id pp.Price_Plan_Id	Trans	Coalesce (pp.Price_Plan_Id, spp.Price_Plan_Id)
CALL_RECORD	Call_Actual_Duration	IN001	CALL_RECORD_TEMP	Call_Actual_Duration	Direct	
CALL_RECORD	Call_Pulse_Charge	IN001	CALL_RECORD_TEMP	Call_Pulse_Charge	Direct	
CALL_RECORD	Call_Charge_Amt	IN001	CALL_RECORD_TEMP	Call_Charge_Amt	Direct	
CALL_RECORD	Call_Ending_Balance	IN001	CALL_RECORD_TEMP	Call_Ending_Balance	Direct	
CALL_RECORD	Call_Result_Code	IN001	Call_Result_Cd	Call_Result_Cd	LookUp	

LEFT JOIN Price_Plan PP ON PP.Price_Plan_Name = CRT.ppl AND CRT.pplan IS NOT NULL LEFT JOIN Subscriber_Price_Plan SPP ON SPP.Subscriber_Id = CRT.Calling_Number AND SPP.End_Dt is null LEFT JOIN CALL_RESULT CR ON CR.Call_Result_Name = CRT.Termination_Reason

TRN CAT, Transformation Category.

COUNTRY

Country_Key
Country_Code Country_Name Country_Description Country_Valid_Flag

Figure 12.15 Target table for the reference data scenario.

For example, if these codes are handled manually, then data mapper Mr. X will assign code 1 to country USA. Assume that Mr. X leaves the project and is replaced by Mr. Y. When the source sends Country Code = USA next month and if Mr. Y is not aware of USA, then he will assign a new code to US, thus creating a duplicate in the reference data. Eventually, business users will see two countries in the report—US and USA.

If these codes are handled automatically, that is, through surrogate keys, then the data warehouse might get populated with garbage data, and business users might see 500 countries and start wondering where they came from.

Source
In this scenario, we will consider two sources for country data.

Target
See Figure 12.15.

Mapping
For this mapping, we have loaded the main data from the file provided by the data steward and then complemented it with source data. Note that the negative system will update any data in the target, but it will only do an insert if it is unable to find that particular country code in the target table.

We added a flag that will tell us whether this country code came from a valid source (1) or from the source system (0).

Make sure that you put all kinds of cleansing rules on source values to ensure that valid LOOKING data is loaded in the target table (Table 12.18).

Table 12.18 Data Mapping for the Reference Data Scenario

Target Table	Target Column	Record Id	Source Table	Source Column	TRN CAT*	Transformation Rule
COUNTRY		REF001	Reference_Data_Lab		+	Generate country keys based on Country_Cd from source. If a row already exists in target then check value of Country Valid Flag; if 1 then do nothing else updated non-pk columns with source values
COUNTRY	Country Key	REF001	Reference_Data_Lab		Trans	
COUNTRY	Country Code	REF001	Reference_Data_Lab	Country_Cd	Direct	
COUNTRY	Country Name	REF001	Reference_Data_Lab	Country_Name	Direct	
COUNTRY	Country Description	REF001	Reference_Data_Lab	Country_Alternate_Name	Direct	
COUNTRY	Country Valid Flag	REF001	CONSTANT	"1"	Hardcode	– 1 for Valid country codes defined by Data Steward
COUNTRY		REF001	Warranty_Claim		–	Select only those values that have alphabet values count 3. Clean data based on column level rule. If this country code is not found in target then insert a new row by giving a new key. Do not update any row in target form this source
COUNTRY	Country Key	REF001	Warranty_Claim		Trans	
COUNTRY	Country Code	REF001	Warranty_Claim	Country	Trans	Use TRIM(UPPER(Country)). Remove any other numeric or characters from data like, _ "etc."
COUNTRY	Country Name	REF001	Warranty_Claim	Country	Direct	
COUNTRY	Country Description	REF001	Warranty_Claim	Country	Direct	
COUNTRY	Country Valid Flag	REF001	CONSTANT	'0'	Hardcode	– 0 for country codes coming from transactional source systems

*TRN CAT: Transformation Category.

One good practice while loading data into reference and surrogate, key, or helping tables is to insert a row with:

Key value = −1
Code/Name/Description = UNKNOWN

During data loading, when the source table is joined with the above tables, nulls can be coalesced with "unknown." Doing this will yield two benefits:

1. Replacing nulls will improve join performance.
2. Key value of −1 in the EDW will help the access layer identify which values were missing in the source data.

BUSINESS KEY, SURROGATE, OR HELPING TABLE WITH MULTIPLE UNIQUE IDS FOR THE SAME LOGICAL CONCEPT

Normally, if we have two unique identifications for the same logical concept, we can store the primary ID in the main table (e.g., PARTY) and its other unique value in the identification table (e.g., PARTY IDENTIFICATION).

However, there would be cases when a logical concept may have two unique identifications. Different source systems might use either one of them. In such a case, there will be at least one source that may provide a relationship between the two unique identifications.

Source

Let's take the example of telecom client. Let's assume that there are two unique values for every product that a user can subscribe to. For example, a package of "100 free minutes" has a unique ID in the Session Initiation Protocol (SIP) system as well as in the IN system. At the same time, the data warehouse receives a daily dump that signifies a relationship between the SIP and IN codes.

Target

Toward the target end of this data, we have a surrogate table that maintains the relationship between both codes. Whereas Prod_Subscription will store data of subscriptions by users, Call_Product will store products that were used in the call (e.g., "free minutes," "main balance account," or "product") (Figure 12.16).

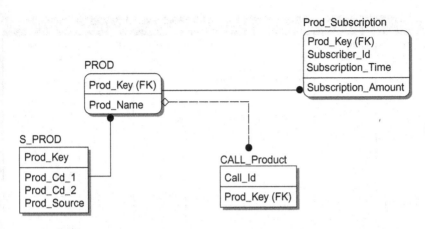

Figure 12.16 Target table for the multiple-identification surrogate scenario.

Mapping

The first two mappings below are connected to loading data in the S_PROD table, where we are storing the relationship between both codes.

Mapping 1

As seen in Table 12.19, we are inserting a complete relationship from the daily dump and only the PROD_CD_1 from the secondary source. We will be using PROD_CD_1 to generate keys and treat PROD_CD_2 as secondary/non-pk column. We don't have any third source. The daily dump will insert and update data, but PROD_SUBSCRIPTION will only insert rows (Table 12.19).

Mapping 2

Here we have a mapping for product subscriptions where the subscription data of these products is loaded. This is the source that is providing the main SIP_Id without any issues so far (Table 12.20).

Mapping 3

Here we are getting the IN product ID, which is the secondary ID in our surrogate or helping table. We cannot generate a new ID for the IN product ID because there is a chance that the same product might end up having two keys in this table: one for the SIP code and the other for the IN code.

Table 12.19 Data Mapping for the Multiple-Identification Surrogate Scenario 1						
Target Table	Target Column	Record Id	Source Table	Source Column	TRN CAT*	Transformation Rule
S_PROD		DUM001	Daily_Dump		+	Generate new key based on Prod_Cd_1 If a row is found in target with Prod_Source <> 1 then update that row from this mapping
S_PROD	Prod_Key	DUM001	ETL		Trans	Generate new key based on Prod_Cd_1
S_PROD	Prod_Cd_1	DUM001	Daily_Dump	SIP_Key	Direct	
S_PROD	Prod_Cd_2	DUM001	Daily_Dump	IN_Key	Direct	
S_PROD	Prod_Source	DUM001	CONSTANT	"1"	Hardcode	− 1 for daily dump
S_PROD		IN001	Prod_Subscription		+	Generate new key based on Prod_Cd_1. Insert only, do not update any row from this source
S_PROD	Prod_Key	IN001	ETL		Trans	Generate new key based on Prod_Cd_1
S_PROD	Prod_Cd_1	IN001	Prod_Subscription	ProdId	Direct	
S_PROD	Prod_Cd_2	IN001	CONSTANT	"Dummy"	Hardcode	
S_PROD	Prod_Source	IN001	CONSTANT	"2"	Hardcode	− 2 for transactional source
*TRN CAT, Transformation Category.						

We will create an orphan table that will be used to keep data whenever the product ID is missing in the surrogate table so that data is populated from this temporary table back into the main table (Figure 12.17).

Mapping

There are three mappings; the main mapping does the transformation based on rules. Two other mappings will handle the product code issue (Table 12.21).

Table 12.20 Data Mapping for the Multiple-Identification Surrogate Scenario 2

Target Table	Target Column	Record Id	Source Table	Source Column	TRN CAT*	Transformation Rule
PROD_SUB		IN001	Prod_Subscription		+	From Prod_Subscription PS left join S_PROD SP ON PS.prodid = SP.Prod_Cd_1
PROD_SUB	Prod_Key	IN001	S_PROD SP	SP_Prod_Key	Direct	
PROD_SUB	Subscriber_Id	IN001	Prod_Subscription	MSISDN	Direct	
PROD_SUB	Subscription_Time	IN001	Prod_Subscription	tm_Stamp	Direct	
PROD_SUB	Subscription_Amount	IN001	Prod_Subscription	Amount	Direct	

*TRN CAT: Transformation Category.

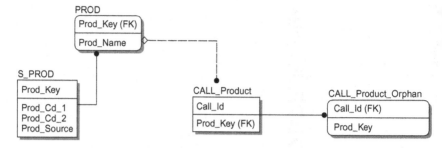

Figure 12.17 Target table for the multiple-identification surrogate scenario with orphan table.

Table 12.21 Data Mapping for the Multiple-Identification Surrogate Scenario with Orphan Table						
Target Table	Target Column	Record Id	Source Table	Source Column	TRN CAT*	Transformation Rule
Call		IN001	Call_Orphan		+	
Call	Call_Id	IN001	Call_Orphan	Call_Id	Direct	
Call	Prodid	IN001	Call_Orphan	Prodid	Direct	
Call_Product		IN001	Call		+	From Prod_Subscription PS left join S_PROD SP ON coalesce (PS.prodid, 'UNKNOWN') = SP. Prod_Cd_2. Insert only those rows which have either a valid value form S_PROD or source is giving NULLs
Call_Product	Call_Id	IN001	Call	Call_id		
Call_Product	Prod_Key	IN001	S_PROD SP	SP. Prod_Key	Direct	
Call_Orphan		IN001	Call_Product		+	Empty this table and insert data where coallesce (prodid,'unknown') not in (sel prod_cd_2 from s_prod)
Call_Orphan	Call_Id	IN001	Call_Product	Call_Id	Direct	
Call_Orphan	Prodid	IN001	Call_Product	Prodid	Direct	
*TRN CAT, Transformation Category.						

The first mapping will run daily before the main mapping such that it loads orphan records within "staging" from the previous run. When the first mapping is executed, the main mapping will be executed, and afterward, the last mapping will load orphan records to the CALL ORPHAN table.

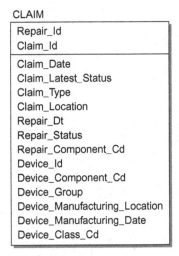

CLAIM

| Repair_Id |
| Claim_Id |
| Claim_Date |
| Claim_Latest_Status |
| Claim_Type |
| Claim_Location |
| Repair_Dt |
| Repair_Status |
| Repair_Component_Cd |
| Device_Id |
| Device_Component_Cd |
| Device_Group |
| Device_Manufacturing_Location |
| Device_Manufacturing_Date |
| Device_Class_Cd |

Figure 12.18 Target table for the denormalized data scenario.

DENORMALIZED OR DATA MART TABLE

A denormalized table contains violations of the third normal form (3NF) and is usually created during physical data modeling. Such a type of tables provides better performance and reduces the number of additional joins considerably.

This is also true in the case of data marts. Sometimes we load data directly from "staging" into the "data mart," the latter of which is mostly denormalized.

Source
The source for this scenario is warranty claims. Consider warranty claims that have multiple attributes of claim themselves plus attributes coming from the device that is being repaired.

Target
In the 3NF model, attributes that are related to a device will be loaded in the DEVICE table, and attributes that are related to the claim itself will be loaded in the CLAIM table. The reason for this step is that multiple repair attempts on the same device may create redundancy in the main table (Figure 12.18).

Mapping
See Table 12.22.

Table 12.22 Data Mapping for the Denormalized Data Scenario

Target Table	Target Column	Record Id	Source Table	Source Column	TRN CAT*	Transformation Rule
CLAIM		CLA001	Warranty_Event Repair_Event Manuf_Det		+	Three source tables will be joined together to populate this tables data. Main table is **WARRANTY_EVENT**, which will be joined with other two using LEFT OUTER JOIN. It is agreed with source that they will send a row in main table whenever either of three tables have new/updated data. Warranty_event WE left join Repair_Event RE ON WE.Warranty_Cd = RE.Warranty_Cd LEFT JOIN Manuf_Det MD ON WE. Mobile_IMEI = MD.IMEI
CLAIM	Claim Id	CLA001	Warranty_Event	Warranty_Cd	Direct	
CLAIM	Repair Id	CLA001	Repair_Event	Warranty_Repair_Cd	Direct	
CLAIM	Claim Date	CLA001	Warranty_Event	Date_Submmited	Direct	
CLAIM	Claim Latest Status	CLA001	Warranty_Event	Warranty_Submitted_Status	Direct	
CLAIM	Claim Type	CLA001	CONSTANT	"1"	Hardcode	– 1 for warranty claim of mobile
CLAIM	Claim Location	CLA001	Warranty_Event	Store_Id	Direct	
CLAIM	Repair Dt	CLA001	Repair_Event	Date_Repaired	Direct	
CLAIM	Repair Status	CLA001	Repair_Event	Status	Direct	

CLAIM	Repair Component Cd	CLA001	Repair_Event	Component_Repaired	Direct
CLAIM	Device Id	CLA001	Warranty_Event	Mobile_IMEI	Direct
CLAIM	Device Component Cd	CLA001	Manuf_Det	Manuf_Component_Cd	Direct
CLAIM	Device Group	CLA001	Manuf_Det	Component_Group	Direct
CLAIM	Device Manufacturing Location	CLA001	Manuf_Det	Factory	Direct
CLAIM	Device Manufacturing Date	CLA001	Manuf_Det	Manuf_date	Direct
CLAIM	Device Class Cd	CLA001	Manuf_Det	Component_Class	Direct

*TRN CAT, Transformation Category.

ACCESS, SEMANTIC, OR PRESENTATION LAYER ATTRIBUTES MAPPING

Consider a scenario in which starting from the loading of data from the source until the actual generation of business reports takes a long time, and the solution architect would like to reduce the execution time. There may be some solutions that could be implemented in the source matrix (SMX) to reduce the execution time pertaining to the semantic or access layer. Because SMX rules are usually executed on delta loads, the rules run faster when applied on smaller datasets.

Source

Let's take the example of a warranty claim when a cell phone is brought to a repair shop. There is a business requirement to find out the first date on which the phone was brought to the shop for repair. There can be multiple repairs on the same device.

Target

The target table in this case is the same (i.e., CLAIM with an additional column of Claim_First_Repair_Flag) (Figure 12.19).

Mapping

See Table 12.23. In the above mapping, we will track a device's first claim by checking its dates during the loading process. Because the daily delta load is much smaller than the historical data, it will be

Figure 12.19 Target table for the semantic layer scenario.

Table 12.23 Data Mapping for the Semantic Layer Scenario

Target Table	Target Column	Record Id	Source Table	Source Column	TRN CAT*	Transformation Rule
CLAIM		CLA001	Warranty_Event Repair_Event Manuf_Det		+	Three source tables joined together to populate this table's data. Main table is WARRANTY_EVENT, which will be joined with other two using LEFT OUTER JOIN. It is agreed with source that they will send a row in main table whenever either of three tables have new/updated data. Warranty_event WE left join Repair_Event RE ON WE.Warranty_Cd = RE.Warranty_Cd LEFT JOIN Manuf_Det MD ON WE. Mobile_IMEI = MD.IMEI LEFT JOIN EDW.CLAIM C ON WE.Mobile_IMEI = C.Device_Id
CLAIM	Claim Id	CLA001	Warranty_Event	Warranty_Cd	Direct	
CLAIM	Repair Id	CLA001	Repair_Event	Warranty_Repair_Cd	Direct	

CLAIM	Claim_First_Repair_Flag	CLA001	EDW_Claim	Claim Date	Trans	CASE
						    WHEN C.DEVICE_ID IS NULL
						        THEN 1
						    WHEN WE.Date_Submitted < C.
						Claim_Date
						        THEN 1
						        ELSE 0
						END
						Update Previous CLAIM by flag = 0 if source provided claim's date is less than EDW claim.

(Continued)

Table 12.23 (Continued)

Target Table	Target Column	Record Id	Source Table	Source Column	TRN CAT*	Transformation Rule
CLAIM	Claim Date	CLA001	Warranty_Event	Date_Submitted	Direct	
CLAIM	Claim Latest Status	CLA001	Warranty_Event	Warranty_Submitted_Status	Direct	
CLAIM	Claim Type	CLA001	CONSTANT	"1"	Hardcode	– 1 for warranty claim of mobile
CLAIM	Claim Location	CLA001	Warranty_Event	Store_Id	Direct	
CLAIM	Repair Dt	CLA001	Repair_Event	Date_Repaired	Direct	
CLAIM	Repair Status	CLA001	Repair_Event	Status	Direct	
CLAIM	Repair Component Cd	CLA001	Repair_Event	Component_Repaired	Direct	
CLAIM	Device Id	CLA001	Warranty_Event	Mobile_IMEI	Direct	
CLAIM	Device Component Cd	CLA001	Manuf_Det	Manuf_Component_Cd	Direct	
CLAIM	Device Group	CLA001	Manuf_Det	Component_Group	Direct	
CLAIM	Device Manufacturing Location	CLA001	Manuf_Det	Factory	Direct	
CLAIM	Device Manufacturing Date	CLA001	Manuf_Det	Manuf_date	Direct	
CLAIM	Device Class Cd	CLA001	Manuf_Det	Component_Class	Direct	

*TRN CAT, Transformation Category.

easier to set the flag during the transformation process rather than doing it in the access layer.

An extra join with the target table is required to extract old claims for the same device. After applying the join, the flag is set for new and old claims.

DIMENSIONS MAPPING

Most of the smaller companies prefer data marts because of their framework based on the star schema or something similar. In such cases, dimensions are built separately to provide a way to look at various facts.

Source
Take the example of the country dimension in which we have multiple source tables that are combined to build a single dimension table.

Target
See Figure 12.20.

Mapping
In most cases, dimensional data will not maintain history (i.e., any change coming from the source will override the old value) (Table 12.24). But if there is a need to track all changes from the country, we can change this mapping to SCD logic. In such cases, the usage of this dimension will be different.

For tracking history, we added start and end date columns in the COUNTRY table and can now track history of any change in nonpk columns. Now when we join a fact with this dimension, we need to provide a date to find the correct time window.

COUNTRY

Country_Cd
Country_Name
Country_Continent
Country_Region
Country_GDP_CLASS
Country_Poverty_Index

Figure 12.20 Target table for the dimension scenario.

Table 12.24 Data Mapping for the Dimension Scenario

Target Table	Target Column	Record Id	Source Table	Source Column	TRN CAT*	Transformation Rule
COUNTRY		DIM001	Country Cntry_Cont Cntry_GDP Cntry_Pow		+	Join all four source tables using full outer join after removing duplicates using qualify ( ) = 1. Once dataset is prepared, join this dataset with target/final table and find rows that already exist in target. If row doesn't exist in target then insert the new row, if it doesn't then update target table and updated only those columns for which we have a not null and valid data from source.
COUNTRY	Country_Cd	DIM001	Country	Cntry_Cd	Direct	
COUNTRY	Country_Name	DIM001	Country	Cntry_Name	Direct	
COUNTRY	Country_Continent	DIM001	Cntry_Cont	Cntry_Continent	Direct	
COUNTRY	Country_Region	DIM001	Country	Region	Direct	
COUNTRY	Country_GDP_Class	DIM001	Cntry_GDP	GDP_Class	Direct	
COUNTRY	Country_Poverty_Index	DIM001	Cntry_Pow	Poverty_Index	Direct	

*TRN CAT: Transformation Category.

```
SELECT *
FROM fact f
INNER JOIN Country d
ON f.country_id = d.County_Id
WHERE f.fact_date BETWEEN d.Effective_Start_Date AND
d.Effective_End_Date
```

APPLY LOGIC VERSUS TRANSFORMATION LOGIC

When we transform data from the source to the target, two steps are involved.

1. Data transformation from the source
2. Data application to the target (Figure 12.21)

In most cases, the data mapper can write rules about data transformation for every mapping and provide a single data application rule for the whole project. For example, a generic data application rule can be "Update old data and insert new rows based on the primary key of the table."

Based on the project's requirements, the above rule can be modified as required. However, there are special cases when the data mapper should define separate rules for both steps. They can be in single mapping with complete details or description provided in the header.

Usually a special apply rule is needed in the below cases:

1. Mapping aggregate data
2. Special update logic is required

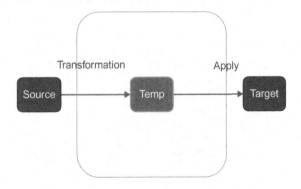

Figure 12.21 Data flow from the staging table to the target table.

3. Special data quality rules
4. Performance issues

DIVIDING THE DATASET INTO SMALLER CHUNKS

We discussed a performance improvement mapping at the start of this chapter in which we divided a single mapping into two mappings. Another approach to improving performance could be to divide source data into smaller chunks.

Source

In this case, let's take an example of financial data; our source table is accounts_transaction containing a bank's daily ledger transactions. The source contains account number, time of transaction, type of transaction, amount, and other columns related to bank account transactions.

Target

See Figure 12.22.

Mapping

When thinking of dividing a large dataset to smaller ones, many techniques and methods may be used. We can divide based on date and time, or we can divide based on type columns. Whatever division technique we use, the resulting datasets should be equally sized to get the benefits of performance improvement.

Apart from equal-sized datasets, we should also ensure the mapping's logic is not impacted, especially when mapping contains

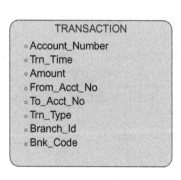

Figure 12.22 Target table for the source-data division into smaller datasets.

aggregate functions. For such cases, use the partitioning column to divide source data into smaller chunks.

Here we will use a technique that is useful for worst-case scenarios for better understanding of the concept. We will use an account number for dividing the source data. After we have done our column-level analysis, we can confirm the below parameters:

```
Data type: Alphanumeric
Null count: 0
Max length: 11
Min length: 7
Total count: 127,000,000
Distinct acct_No: 49,000,000
Average rows per val: 2.17
```

The above statistics are very important to understand each column's content; we have enough information to decide when making the division. The minimum length of the column is 6, and there are no nulls in this column; this means that if we use any of the first 6 characters for the formula, we won't face any problems. Let's take the third character of the column for this example. Before we create mappings, we need to verify the division of the target dataset. Run the below query to see the size of resulting datasets.

```
SELECT SUBSTRING( Account_Number ,3,1) as Val, COUNT(*) as Row_Count
FROM ACCOUNT_TRANSACTIONS
GROUP BY SUBSTRING( Account_Number ,3,1)
```

Table 12.25 shows the resulting dataset for the above query. The above data is fairly even, giving almost equal datasets. But looking at the values, we can notice only 12 characters from both alphabets and numbers. Does this mean that there can be other characters in the future?

When creating a mapping, we need to cover all possible future scenarios; we can do this by requesting the client to provide detailed information about account number creation logic. Second, we should always create an extra group for "other" values to accommodate data that might come in the future (Table 12.26).

Table 12.25 Datasets Based on the Third Alphabet of Column Value	
Val	**Row_Count**
a	21166666
b	10583333
c	20583333
d	40583333
y	10583333
z	583333
1	10583337
2	30583333
3	83333
4	10583333
5	10583333
6	10583333

UNSTRUCTURED DATA

Data warehousing normally deals with structured data in the form of relational databases, but there can be special cases in which we come across unstructured data. There is a separate field of big data that deals with unstructured data; the techniques deal specifically with data in an unstructured format.

Even though data comes in an unstructured format, there is always some level of connection in this data. We can exploit this connection and convert the source data into table form.

Source

In the below example, we will discuss one such scenario where the source is sending random rows in a file. However, there is a sequence in receiving rows, and it is always followed. Below is the file format:

- User's data: 7 values separated by "|"
- Header data: 21 values separated by ","
- Form filling success flag: 2 values separated by ";"
- Form's fields data: 6 values separated by "$"

The last row in the above sequence can be repeated multiple times with a limit of five times. This presents a major challenge for the data mapper—how to convert this sequence into row format. For one, if

Table 12.26 Data Mapping for Source-Data Division Into Smaller Datasets

Target Table	Target Column	Record Id	Source Table	Source Column	TRN CAT*	Transformation Rule
TRN		TRN1	Account_Trn		+	Filter Data on below condition WHERE SUBSTRING(account,3,1) = 'a'
TRN	Acc_No	TRN1	Account_Trn	Account	Direct	
TRN	Time	TRN1	Account_Trn	Time	Direct	
TRN	……	TRN1				
TRN		TRN2	Account_Trn		+	Filter Data on below condition WHERE SUBSTRING(account,3,1) = 'b'
TRN	Acc_No	TRN2	Account_Trn	Account	Direct	
TRN	Time	TRN2	Account_Trn	Time	Direct	
TRN	……	TRN2				
TRN		TRN3	Account_Trn		+	Filter Data on below condition WHERE SUBSTRING(account,3,1) = 'c'
TRN	Acc_No	TRN3	Account_Trn	Account	Direct	
TRN	Time	TRN3	Account_Trn	Time	Direct	
TRN	……	TRN3				
TRN		TRN4	Account_Trn		+	Filter Data on below condition WHERE SUBSTRING(account,3,1) = 'd'
TRN	Acc_No	TRN4	Account_Trn	Account	Direct	
TRN	Time	TRN4	Account_Trn	Time	Direct	
TRN	……	TRN4				

(Continued)

Table 12.26 (Continued)

Target Table	Target Column	Record Id	Source Table	Source Column	TRN CAT*	Transformation Rule
TRN		TRN5	Account_Trn		+	Filter Data on below condition WHERE SUBSTRING(account,3,1) = 'y'
TRN	Acc_No	TRN5	Account_Trn	Account	Direct	
TRN	Time	TRN5	Account_Trn	Time	Direct	
TRN	……..	TRN5				
TRN		TRN6	Account_Trn		+	Filter Data on below condition WHERE SUBSTRING(account,3,1) = 'z'
TRN	Acc_No	TRN6	Account_Trn	Account	Direct	
TRN	Time	TRN6	Account_Trn	Time	Direct	
TRN	……..	TRN6				
TRN		TRN7	Account_Trn		+	Filter Data on below condition WHERE SUBSTRING(account,3,1) = "1"
TRN	Acc_No	TRN7	Account_Trn	Account	Direct	
TRN	Time	TRN7	Account_Trn	Time	Direct	
TRN	……..	TRN7				
TRN		TRN8	Account_Trn		+	Filter Data on below condition WHERE SUBSTRING(account,3,1) = "2"
TRN	Acc_No	TRN8	Account_Trn	Account	Direct	
TRN	Time	TRN8	Account_Trn	Time	Direct	
TRN	……..	TRN8				
TRN		TRN9	Account_Trn		+	Filter Data on below condition WHERE SUBSTRING(account,3,1) = "3"

TRN CAT	Field	TRN	Account_Trm	Account/Time	Direct/+	Note
TRN	Acc_No	TRN9	Account_Trm	Account	Direct	
TRN	Time	TRN9	Account_Trm	Time	Direct	
TRN	....	TRN9				
TRN		TRN10	Account_Trm		+	Filter Data on below condition WHERE SUBSTRING(account,3,1) = '4'
TRN	Acc_No	TRN10	Account_Trm	Account	Direct	
TRN	Time	TRN10	Account_Trm	Time	Direct	
TRN	....	TRN10				
TRN		TRN11	Account_Trm		+	Filter Data on below condition WHERE SUBSTRING(account,3,1) = '5'
TRN	Acc_No	TRN11	Account_Trm	Account	Direct	
TRN	Time	TRN11	Account_Trm	Time	Direct	
TRN	....	TRN11				
TRN		TRN12	Account_Trm		+	Filter Data on below condition WHERE SUBSTRING(account,3,1) = '6'
TRN	Acc_No	TRN12	Account_Trm	Account	Direct	
TRN	Time	TRN12	Account_Trm	Time	Direct	
TRN	....	TRN12				
TRN		TRN13	Account_Trm		+	Filter Data on below condition WHERE SUBSTRING(account,3,1) not in ("a","b","c","d","y","z","0","1","2","3","4","5","6")
TRN	Acc_No	TRN13	Account_Trm	Account	Direct	
TRN	Time	TRN13	Account_Trm	Time	Direct	
TRN	....	TRN13				

*TRN CAT, Transformation Category.

the row starts with an identifier, then we can join both datasets together using this identifier.

Target
For this example, we only convert the source data into tabular form.

Mapping
Because we know that the delimiter in each case is different, we can use a combination of the SUBSTRING and INDEX function to count occurrences of this delimiter. If the count and delimiter match the above explanation, then we can add another column in the table to mark the type of row.

Load this data into a table and add a row number column giving the data's sequence in the file. This will result in two columns of the table: one will be row number, and the other will hold actual data (Table 12.27).

Next we can convert source data into a single format by using a single delimiter for all types of rows; this will help later on in separating one column into multiple columns (Table 12.28).

Table 12.27 Data Mapping for the Unstructured Data Scenario 1					
Target Table	**Target Column**	**Source Table**	**Source Column**	**TRN CAT***	**Transformation Rule**
FormData_2		FormData_1		+	
FormData_2	Row#	FormData_1	Row#	Direct	
FormData_2	Data	FormData_1	Data	Direct	
FormData_2	Type	FormData_1		Transf	Count number of delimiter values. If delimiter = "|" and count > = 7 then "U" If delimiter = "," and count > = 21 then "H" If delimiter = ";" and count > = 2 then "F" If delimiter = "$" and count > = 6 then "T"
TRN CAT, Transformation Category.					

Target Table	Target Column	Source Table	Source Column	TRN CAT*	Transformation Rule
FormData_3		FormData_2		+	
FormData_3	Row#	FormData_2	Row#	Direct	
FormData_3	Data	FormData_2	Data	Trans	Change delimiter to "|" for all data
FormData_3	Type	FormData_2	Type	Direct	

Table 12.28 Data Mapping for the Unstructured Data Scenario 2

TRN CAT, Transformation Category.

The last thing we need to do is to convert all types of rows into a single row and column format. For this, we will use self-joins multiple times. We have a sequence number of row in the file and type of row; by using these two, we can transpose the data based on our requirements.

```
SELECT U.data +' |' + H.data +' |' + F.data +' |' + T1.data
  FROM
    FormData_3 U
  JOIN FormData_3 H
  ON U.row# + 1 = H.row#
AND H.Type =' H'
JOIN FormData_3 F
  ON U.row# + 2 = F.row#
AND F.Type =' F'
JOIN FormData_3 T1
ON
(
    U.row# + 3 = T1.row#
OR U.row# + 4 = T1.row#
OR U.row# + 5 = T1.row#
OR U.row# + 6 = T1.row#
OR U.row# + 7 = T1.row#
)
AND T1.Type =' T'
WHERE U.type = 'U'
```

The above transformation will return one column containing the data of the whole row but in the same format. Now we can convert this single column to multiple columns by using a delimiter.

DATA TRANSPOSE

Transpose in data warehousing is defined as converting a table's columns to rows or rows to columns. This kind of transformation is usually done to either normalize source data or to denormalize.

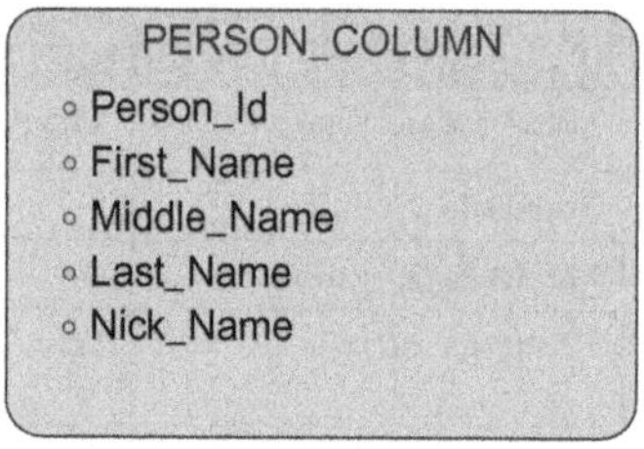

Figure 12.23 Source data for the data transpose scenario.

Figure 12.24 Target table for the data transpose scenario.

Source

Because we will explain both types of transposes, the below source will also act as the target. Consider a source that stores names in column format (Figure 12.23).

Target

Our target table contains the Name_Type column, which distinguishes among different names (Figure 12.24).

Mapping

Transpose: Converting Columns to Rows

For converting columns into rows, we can simply use the UNION function to merge each column's data one by one. We can also implement column-level rules if required, although this is a straightforward data union.

```
SELECT A.Person_id, 'First Name' as Name_Type, COALESCE
(First_Name,' Not Available in Source' ) as Name_Value
FROM PERSON_COLUMN
UNION ALL
```

```
SELECT A.Person_id, 'Middle Name' as Name_Type, COALESCE
(Middle_Name,' Not Available in Source' ) as Name_Value
FROM PERSON_COLUMN
UNION ALL
SELECT A.Person_id, 'Last Name' as Name_Type, COALESCE
(Last_Name,' Not Available in Source' ) as Name_Value
FROM PERSON_COLUMN
UNION ALL
SELECT A.Person_id, 'Nick Name' as Name_Type, COALESCE
(Nick_Name,' Not Available in Source' ) as Name_Value
FROM PERSON_COLUMN
```

We are using UNION ALL because we are 100% sure that all four datasets are mutually exclusive and will not result in a duplicate value by using a hard-coded value for the NAME_TYPE column and give a unique value to each dataset. If there was a possibility of a full-row duplicate, we would have used the UNION function instead of UNION ALL.

Transpose: Converting Rows to Columns

For converting rows into columns, we will use self-join on the primary key and select one column from each joining dataset. We will use a full outer join to make sure that we don't lose any data because of a missing name.

```
SELECT COALESCE (A.Person_Id,B.Person_Id,C.Person_Id,D.Person_Id)
AS Person_Id,
  A.Name_Value AS First_Name
  , B.Name_Value AS Middle_Name
  , C.Name_Value AS Last_Name
  , D.Name_Value AS Nick_Name
FROM PERSON_ROWS A
FULL OUTER JOIN PERSON_ROWS B
ON A.Person_Id = B.Person_Id
FULL OUTER JOIN PERSON_ROWS C
ON A.Person_Id = C.Person_Id
FULL OUTER JOIN PERSON_ROWS D
ON A.Person_Id = D.Person_Id
WHERE A.Name_Type = 'First Name'
AND B.Name_Type = 'Middle Name'
AND C.Name_Type = 'Last Name'
AND D.Name_Type = 'Nick Name'
```

Interestingly, the number of columns in the target case is limited; hence, this kind of self-join works fine, and we don't have to work with recursive queries in this case.

AGGREGATE FUNCTIONS AND LOADING CYCLE

Aggregate functions can be used in mappings and require careful analysis of grouping and portioning columns to ensure that the resulting aggregated value is correct. The result can be wrong if data is distributed in multiple extracts and processes separately.

Some aggregate functions are easier to load than others. For example, the SUM function can be used without special rules; the data mapper can add the SUMed value of the current extract into the target table's old value. However, some functions such as AVERAGE can give wrong results if we don't handle the logic in transformation.

For functions such as AVERAGE, if all data is processed in one cycle, then the aggregated value will be correct. But if we are taking the average of the data from two different days, then the result will be wrong if we don't apply special logic.

Source
In this scenario, we will take some retail store data as the source. In the source data, we have daily transactions of a retail store's different branches, giving information about time, product, price, and so on.

Because of the large amount of data, the data warehouse will process the source data once every hour. This means that the same date's data will be processed 24 times in a single day.

Target
In the target, we are storing sales of the store in aggregated form (Figure 12.25).

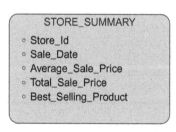

Figure 12.25 Target table for the complex aggregation scenario.

Apart from the first two columns, all other columns in the target require aggregate functions. We will load data from this source once every hour, resulting in the same date's data being processed in different batches. If we don't apply a special rule here, the old value will be replaced by the new value, giving the wrong results. Instead, we should store all values that are calculated for all rows of a particular store on a particular date.

Mapping

Below are different options to handle such situations.

Store Raw Data Separately

One way to get correct results in the aggregated function is to use a temporary table before loading complete data in the final table. The idea here is to store raw source data in its original form in a temporary table and then use the aggregate function on top of this table, loading the resultset in the final table.

The benefit of having this extra table is that our results will be correct. However, it also requires overhead for managing and storing data.

The performance of the system can be improved by regularly removing old data that is not of interest. For example, we can backdate data to a maximum of 5 days; this means that all data before the past 5 days will be deleted from the temporary table. This will save disk space and speed up performance.

Performance can be further improved by having the same index of the temporary and final table and by partitioning the temporary table. With partitions defined, we will join new extract data with the temporary table and process only the required data.

Step 1: Insert new data from the source to the temporary table.
Step 2: Calculate the aggregates and insert data into the final table. To reduce the amount of data that is being processed, we will add a filter condition.

```
SELECT store_id, sale_Date, sum(amount)/count(*)
FROM TEMP
WHERE (store_id, sale_Date) IN
(
  SELECT store_id, sale_date
  FROM Sales_Source
  GROUP BY store_id, sale_date
)
```

Table 12.29 Target Table Snapshot Before Loading				
Store_Id	Date	Average_Sale	Sale_Amount	Sale_Count
123	1/13/2016	759	5420089	7138

Table 12.30 Temporary Table Stats Before Apply				
Store_Id	Date	Average_Sale	Sale_Amount	Sale_Count
123	1/13/2016	1469	82250	56

Store Row Count with Aggregated Column

The second option is to store all parameters required for special aggregate function in the target table. For example, in the case of average, we need the SUM of the amount and the total COUNT of rows, and then we will divide SUM with COUNT to get the average.

In this solution, we will store all values in the target table along with the average value for a correct result. Consider the state of the target table before it is loaded (Table 12.29).

From new source data, we have the result shown in Table 12.30 after transformation but before apply. To update the target table with correct stats, we can use the following query.

```
UPDATE target
FROM source
SET Average_Sale = (SOURCE. Sale_Amount + TARGET.Sale_Amount)
/ (SOURCE.Sale_Count + TARGET.Sale_Count)
, Sale_Amount = SOURCE.Sale_Amount + TARGET.Sale_Amount
, Sale_Count = SOURCE.Sale_Count + TARGET.Sale_Count
WHERE SOURCE.Store_Id = TARGET.Store_Id
AND SOURCE.Sale_Date = TARGET.Sale_Date
```

Having additional columns to keep all required parameters of data is mandatory to ensure the correct figure is provided to business users.

INITIAL LOAD VERSUS DELTA LOAD

We write transformation rules for regular data extracts from the source in the data mapping document; this loading cycle is commonly referred to as *delta loading*. When the data warehouse goes to production, we load the history data from the source; this is called the *initial* or *full load*.

The transformation logic of the history data is usually the same unless the source contains multiple releases' data. In the real world, almost every online transaction processing (OLTP) or operational source is modified to add new features or to fix bugs.

Such changes in sources result in data quality or logic issues. When doing the initial load from the source system, the data mapper needs to define special rules for such issues.

Apart from changes in the source system, clients also have legacy sources' data. These systems were replaced by new and better solutions by the client, and the data warehouse has to load data from all sources.

Transformation rules for the initial load should also be documented in the data mapping document. We can add an extra marker column that gives information whether this mapping is for the initial load or the delta load.

RECURSIVE QUERY

The sources of a data warehouse are usually in tabular form, but there can be cases when the data value inside a column contains multiple values without a defined limit. When there is a business requirement to convert this type of data into row form, we have to rely on recursive logic.

Source

The source in this scenario is sales order data, which gives information about order ID, order date, item ordered, and item price (Table 12.31). The problem is that product ID and the price are given in a single column. There are two levels of delimiters in this column: the first delimiter is ":" separating items ordered, and the second delimiter "," separates item ID from its price (Figure 12.26).

Table 12.31 Source Data for the Recursive Query Scenario		
Order_Id	Order_Date	Order_Detail
545	12/17/2015	69127,25.3:35415,598.0:65897,58.9
528	12/16/2015	54544,89.0
559	12/21/2015	45545,9.0:54687,58.9:89654,87.0:40120,6.6:890014,20.2

Target

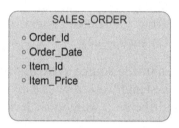

Figure 12.26 Target table for the recursive query scenario.

Mapping

The mapping shown in Table 12.32 explains the recursive logic for the target table.

Apart from separating values inside a column, recursive logic is also required if we are creating rows based on a range. For example, if we have a range of cell phone vouchers from 100 to 1000 and the business requires one row for each voucher, then we have to use a recursive query.

SQL language is not meant for object-oriented programming logic, and recursive queries create major performance issues. A data mapper should use SQL language only if the number of iterations (depth of data in a column) is small relative to the database engine.

If the depth of data is very big and causes system performance issues, then it is recommended to implement recursive logic outside of the database and then load the resultset into the table.

Below is a sample code for recursive queries from Microsoft SQL (MSSQL).

Target Table	Target Column	Source Table	Source Column	TRN CAT*	Transformation Rule
	**Table 12.32 Data Mapping for the Recursive Query Scenario**				
Sales_Order		Orders		+	
Sales_Order	Order_Id	Orders	Order_Id	Direct	
Sales_Order	Order_Date	Orders	Order_Date	Direct	
Sales_Order	Item_Id	Orders	Order_Detail	Transformation	Source column contains multiple rows separated by ":" and each row with two columns separated by "," The first column of this row will be mapped to Item_Id of target table
Sales_Order	Item_Price	Orders	Order_Detail	Transformation	Source column contains multiple rows separated by ":" and each row with two columns separated by "," The second column of this row will be mapped to Item_Price of target table

TRN CAT, Transformation Category.

```
CREATE TABLE Recursive_Table
(
  Primary_Key_Of_Table INT,
  string CHAR(991)
);
INSERT VALUES Recursive_Table VALUES (1, 'a,b,c,d,e');
INSERT VALUES Recursive_Table VALUES (2, 'a,bb,ccc,dddd,eeeee');
WITH RECURSIVE Temporary_Recursive_Table
(Primary_Key_Of_Table,
  Length,
  Remaining_String,
  word,
  Position
) AS (
SELECT
  Primary_Key_Of_Table,
  Find_Position(',' IN String || ',') - 1 AS Length,
  Sub_string(String || ',' FROM Length + 2) AS Remaining_String,
  Sub_string(String FROM 1 FOR Length) AS word,
    1
FROM Recursive_Table
UNION ALL
SELECT
  Primary_Key_Of_Table,
  PositionITION(',' IN Remaining_String) - 1 AS Length_new,
  Sub_string(Remaining_String FROM Length_new + 2),
  Sub_string(Remaining_String FROM 1 FOR Length_new),
```

```
   Position +1
 FROM Temporary_Recursive_Table
 WHERE Remaining_String < > "
)
SELECT
 Primary_Key_Of_Table, Position, word
FROM Temporary_Recursive_Table
Ordering_By_Column Primary_Key_Of_Table, Position;
```

LOADING SEQUENCE OF MAPPING

The data warehouse extracts data from the source and gives final reports to business users. In between these two steps lies a complex data flow logic that moves data from one point to another, transforming it each time to bring it close to the final report.

This transformation of individual datasets can be done in parallel to speed up the loading process, but sometimes we come across cases in which dependency between datasets can create wrong results. For these data mappings, we define the sequence in which data will be transformed and give each mapping a unique sequence number.

This kind of dependency can be between source systems or between mappings of the same source system. The complexity of sequencing can vary based on the client's business model.

If there is dependency between source systems, then we need to implement sequencing in the loading schedule. This can be documented in the data mapping document in a separate worksheet that gives information about the source system scheduling; Table 12.33 is one example.

For dependency within the source system, we can define the sequencing at the mapping level.

Source

Let's take an example of a mobile manufacturing client. The client has a unique identification system called DSN for its devices and gives every device manufactured a unique ID. There is also an international standard for identifying every mobile uniquely. This code is called IMEI.

In this scenario, we have two sources. The first one gives the relationship between DSN and IMEI. The second source gives data about warranty claims, which provides both DSN and IMEI. But most of the time, DSN is either null or contains garbage data.

Table 12.33 Source System Wise Loading Priority or Sequence				
Source System	Frequency	Time	Dependency	Sequence
Source 1	Daily	2:00 AM	N	0
Source 2	Daily	12:00 AM	N	0
Source 3	Daily	12:00 AM	Y	SQ1.2
Source 4	Daily	2:00 AM	Y	SQ1.3
Source 5	Daily	11:00 PM	Y	SQ1.1
Source 6	Monthly	2:00 AM	N	0
Source 7	Monthly	12:00 AM	N	0
Source 8	Daily	12:00 AM	Y	SQ2.1
Source 9	Daily	12:00 AM	Y	SQ2.2
Source 10	Daily	2:00 AM	N	0

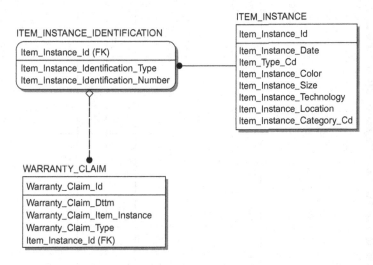

Figure 12.27 Target table for the loading sequence scenario.

In EDW, DSN is used to uniquely identify an instance of a cell phone; hence, it is not acceptable to have nulls or garbage data in this column. Ideally, the source should provide us with this information, but let's assume that this cannot be done.

Target
See Figure 12.27.

Mapping
The sequence number will define which mapping to execute first and which afterward (Table 12.34). In the above case, we want the ITEM INSTANCE IDENTIFICATION table loaded first followed by ITEM INSTANCE and WARRANTY CLAIM last.

Table 12.34 Data Mapping for the Loading Sequence Scenario

Target Table	Target Column	Record Id	Source Table	Source Column	Transformation Rule	Sequence
ITEM INSTANCE IDENTIFICATION		MAN001	MANUF_DETAIL		P = 100	SQMM1.1
ITEM INSTANCE IDENTIFICATION	Item Instance Id	MAN001	MANUF_DETAIL	DSN		
ITEM INSTANCE IDENTIFICATION	Identification Type	MAN001	MANUF_DETAIL	IMEI		
ITEM INSTANCE IDENTIFICATION	Identification Number	MAN001	CONSTANT	"1"	– "1" is for IMEI	
ITEM INSTANCE		CLA001	Claim		P = 30 Join with ITEM INST IDENTIFICATION on SOURCE.IMEI = Item Instance Identification Number and Item Instance Identification Type = 1 If a row is found then ignore this row. Else Insert a row only if DSN column length is greater than 8 and first three characters are alphabets. Use uppercase and trim.	SQMM1.2
ITEM INSTANCE	Item Instance Id	CLA001	Claim	DSN IMEI	UPPER(TRIM(DSN)) See header rule for filtering of data	
ITEM INSTANCE	Item Instance Date	CLA001	Claim	Claim_Dt		
WARRANTY CLAIM		CLA001	Claim		P = 100 CLAIM a Left join ITEM INSTANCE IDENTIFICATION b ON a.IMEI = b. Item Instance Identification Number AND b. Item Instance Identification = 1	SQMM1.3

WARRANTY CLAIM	Warranty Claim Id	CLA001	Claim	Claim_Id	
WARRANTY CLAIM	Warranty Claim Dttm	CLA001	Claim	Claim_Dt	

WARRANTY CLAIM	Item Instance	CLA001	Claim	IMEI/DSN	CASE
					  WHEN B.Item Instance Id IS NOT NULL
					  THEN B.Item Instance Id
					  WHEN length (A. DSN) >8 AND substr
					(A.DSN,1,3) is alphanumeric
					  THEN UPPER(TRIM(DSN))
					  ELSE "UNKNOWN"
					END

WARRANTY CLAIM	Warranty Claim Type	CLA001	CONSTANT	"1"	

Attribute Items that represent a single type of information in a dimension (e.g., year is an attribute in the time dimension)

BI Business intelligence

Data mart A data warehouse with a more limited audience or data content; see data warehouse

Data warehouse A subject-oriented, integrated, time-variant, nonvolatile collection of data in support of management's decision-making process (as defined Inmon, 2002)

Detail transformation document (DTD) Another name for data mapping document. This document contain information about transformation rules of mapping

Dimension The same category of information (e.g., year, month, day, and week are all part of the time dimension)

Extract, transform, load (ETL) The movement of data from one area to another

Fact table A type of table in the dimensional model. A fact table typically includes two types of columns: fact columns and foreign keys to the dimensions.

Initial load The first population of the production database installations using the data acquisition modules for extraction, transformation, and transportation

Logical data model (LDM) Data model of data warehouse giving logical picture of entities and it's relationships

Measure A quantifiable variable or value stored in a multidimensional online analytical processing (OLAP) cube; a value in the cell at the intersection of two or more dimensions

Metadata Data about data (e.g., the number of tables in the database is a type of metadata)

Normalization A technique used to eliminate data redundancy

Physical data model (PDM) Data model giving physical details of data warehouse tables

Primary index An index used to improve performance on the combination of columns most frequently used to access rows in a table

Primary key A set of one or more columns in a database table whose values, in combination, are required to be unique within the table

Relationship What one entity has to do with another; any significant way in which two things of the same or different type may be associated

Row An entry in a table that typically corresponds to an instance of some real thing, consisting of a set of values for all mandatory columns and relevant optional columns; a row is often an implementation of an instance of an entity

Source matrix (SMX) Data mapping document

Snowflake schema A common form of dimensional model; different hierarchies in a dimension can be extended into their own dimensional tables. Therefore, a dimension can have more than a single dimension table.

Star schema A common form of dimensional model; each dimension is represented by a single dimension table

BIBLIOGRAPHY

Giordano, A.D., 2010. Data Integration Blueprint and Modeling: Techniques for a Scalable and Sustainable Architecture. IBM Press, Cranbury, NJ.

Inmon, W.H., 2002. Building the Data Warehouse, third ed. John Wiley & Sons, New York.

Kimball, R., Ross, M., 2002. The Data Warehouse Toolkit: The Complete Guide to Dimensional Modeling, second ed. John Wiley & Sons, New York.

Printed in the United States
By Bookmasters